Transsexuality

Evangelical Alliance
Policy Commission

Copyright © 2000 Evangelical Alliance
Whitefield House, 186 Kennington Park Road, London SE11 4BT

First published in 2000 by Evangelical Alliance Policy Commission

Evangelical Alliance Policy Commission is an imprint of Paternoster Publishing,
PO Box 300, Carlisle, Cumbria CA3 0QS, UK
and Paternoster Publishing USA
Box 1047, Waynesboro, GA 30830–2047
www.paternoster-publishing.com

*All rights reserved. No part of this publication may be reproduced,
stored in a retrieval system, or transmitted, in any form or by any means,
electronic, mechanical, photocopying, recording or otherwise,
without the prior permission of the publisher or a licence permitting restricted copying.
In the UK such licences are issued by the Copyright Licensing Agency,
90 Tottenham Court Road, London W1P 9HE.*

British Library Cataloguing-in-Publication Data

A catalogue record for this book is available from the British Library

ISBN 0–95329–926–0

Unless otherwise stated, Scripture quotations are taken from the
HOLY BIBLE, NEW INTERNATIONAL VERSION
Copyright © 1973, 1978, 1984 by the International Bible Society.
Used by permission of Hodder & Stoughton Ltd. All rights reserved.
'NIV' is a registered trademark of the International Bible Society
UK trademark number 1448790

Typeset by Waverley Typesetters, Galashiels
Cover design by Campsie
Printed and bound in Great Britain by
Cox & Wyman Ltd, Reading, Berkshire

Contents

About the Policy Commission	vii
Foreword	ix
Introduction	xi
1. Transsexuality – Key Definitions and Terminology	1
2. The Current and Historical Contexts	7
3. Medical Considerations Relating to Transsexuality	14
4. Political and Legal Considerations Relating to Transsexuality	29
5. The Perspective of Scripture	45
6. An Ethical Perspective on Transsexuality	55
7. Some Practical and Pastoral Considerations Relating to Transsexuality	71
Conclusion: Affirmations and Recommendations	84
Select Bibliography and Further Reading	88
Useful Addresses of Christian Organisations	89

About the Policy Commission

The Evangelical Alliance's Millennium Manifesto incorporated a decision to create a Policy Commission, which was initiated in 1999. Adopting an evangelical viewpoint, its remit was to identify and recommend policy statements on contemporary and controversial issues – typically of an ethical nature with national or international implications – as distinct from purely theological and doctrinal concerns. Although addressing in the first instance evangelical Christians and churches, its studies are intended to be of wider relevance to the Christian community at large as it seeks to provide a co-ordinated ethical response to matters of wider public debate.

The Policy Commission's Steering Group comprises evangelical representatives from a wide range of academic, scientific and professional disciplines. Its reports are produced following a wide-ranging discussion and consultation process, both internally through the Evangelical Alliance membership, and externally by reference to academics and relevant practitioners in the appropriate fields.

The next report to appear from the Policy Commission will examine the subject of Genetically Modified Foods.

For more information about the Policy Commission write to:

Don Horrocks
Co-ordinator, Policy Commission
Evangelical Alliance
Whitefield House
186 Kennington Park Road
London
SE11 4BT

e-mail:	slegon@eauk.org
Website:	http://www.eauk.org
Telephone:	020 7207 2100
Fax:	020 7207 2150

Foreword

When the Policy Commission decided to submit a report on Transsexuality many of us doubted the wisdom of their choice. After all, there are many other subjects which seemed to be far more pressing for evangelicals; there was no sign of an evangelical stampede coming at us for a rapid response to the subject! In fact, one of our earliest responses to the Commission included a lengthy discussion as to whether the word really had one 's' or two!

Subsequently, two developments have vindicated their choice. The first was the fact that, *Truth on the Streets*, a major presentation in 1999 written for the Evangelical Alliance, highlighted our responses to a number of 'touchy' topics by presenting a Christian transsexual as the major character. The second was the fact that the Commission not only submitted the only *Christian* report to the Home Office's inquiry on the subject, but presented the *only* major submission of its kind to assist policy on the subject.

The fact is that this issue which has lain dormant within the Christian Church is now presenting a steady flow of live examples for local congregations. Whether we like it or not it won't go away.

Inevitably, any attempt to grasp a contentious issue such as this is bound to offend. But that is not the intention. This report, which comes with the endorsement of the Evangelical Alliance

Council, is no anti-transsexual polemic. It recognises the genuine convictions of transsexuals and attempts to handle this complex subject with careful sensitivity. But it also reflects the fact that there is a body of opinion which seeks to balance compassion with truth, and is informed by Biblical convictions.

The report presents an evangelical response to a difficult issue which already exists for individuals in society and which will increasingly affect the life in our churches. For some of us it will be a helpful discussion point. For others it is increasingly likely to be a crucial resource in the immediate future.

Joel Edwards
General Director of the Evangelical Alliance

Introduction

The question may understandably be asked, 'Why a book on such an obscure subject?' Well, during the past few years the issue of transsexuality has become increasingly high profile, not only in the media, but also in the political arena and in the courts where recent employment legislation has been widened to take account of people who are transsexuals. In response to interest group pressure, further government legislation is anticipated soon to address the subject, including, for example, questions of identity and marriage. Groups of Christian transsexual people have also emerged to argue a case for acceptance of their particular lifestyle on biblical and other grounds. In Christian circles, notably in churches, Bible colleges, Christian organisations and national conferences, the question of transsexuality has begun to surface with increasing frequency. It has become such a live and contentious issue amongst Christians – one that involves complex and perplexing practical and theological consequences – that an investigation and response to some of the implications raised is now called for.

Our approach in this book has been to *inform* the Christian public about this little-known subject, *analyse* the issues and implications that arise from a Christian standpoint, and *suggest* guidelines for how a Christian response to transsexual people might work in practice. Although we principally address evangelical churches, we nevertheless consider this study should be of wider use to the Church in general since the issues and dilemmas raised entail common considerations. Our specific aims in setting out a Christian response to transsexual behaviour include:

1. Assisting Christians to respond more effectively to media and interest groups seeking to promote transsexuality as a valid alternative lifestyle by providing an informed resource tool.

2. Assisting Christians in relating pastorally, socially and sensitively to transsexual people whilst upholding biblical standards both of morality and compassion.

3. Affirming and supporting Christians who are actively involved in ministering to those who seek pastoral support as they consider coping with, moving towards, or moving away from, a transsexual lifestyle.

4. Affirming and supporting Christian families where a member has adopted a transsexual lifestyle.

5. Providing a basis for relevant input at Parliamentary level to the legislative and opinion-forming processes.

In terms of scope, this is not intended as an exhaustive scientific study. Rather, it is offering an appropriately comprehensive and comprehensible overview. It is a summary and response to the highly complex subject that has tended until now to be characterised by a general lack of awareness.

For the sake of clarity, the study has been divided into a series of perspectives on the subject – those of medicine and science, politics and law, Scripture, ethics, and a pastoral section for practical guidance. The concluding affirmations represent a considered outlook and advisory guidelines on the question of transsexuality from the standpoint of the Evangelical Alliance. It should be noted that some of the terminology relating to discussion about transsexuality may be both confusing and not without contention. We have therefore provided a guide to the more specialist use of terms within this study on pages 2–6. The approach adopted seeks to be firm in terms of adherence to Christian beliefs, whilst also sensitive, compassionate and non-judgmental in tone. We realise that the subject tends to provoke strong and emotive reactions, and although our stance will seem to oppose certain agendas, our underlying concern is to promote a caring and respectful response to transsexual people from the Christian community.

1

Transsexuality – Key Definitions and Terminology

For the purpose of this study we have chosen to define *sex* as the physical, hormonal and genetic characteristics that differentiate between male and female, whilst *gender* may be seen more as having to do with how people present themselves as masculine or feminine.[1] *Gender identity confusion*, or *gender identity disorder*, are terms used to describe people whose sense of self (identity) is inconsistent with their biological sex. Such people are usually referred to as *transsexual*. Though there are historical examples of gender confusion, the terms *transsexual* and *transvestite* (the latter term referring to people who have a compulsion to cross-dress though not necessarily to identify with the opposite sex) are peculiar to the twentieth century.

We set out below working definitions of the more technical terminology we have employed in this study. It should be noted that there is considerable controversy and difference of opinion in the wider public arena relating to these definitions. Some groups have vested interests in what they would prefer certain categories to be regarded as. Our understanding of the relevant terminology has generally been arrived at following wide consultation and conservative established opinion.

---

1. See pp.55ff.

Gender

To do with how people present themselves as either masculine or feminine. A clinical definition of gender generally accepted today by the medical and para-medical community is: 'That which a person says and does to indicate to oneself and to others the degree to which one is male or female.'[2] A recent popular definition suggests *gender* is a term that is introduced 'to distinguish physically determined sex from psychologically perceived sexual status'.[3] *Gender identity* refers to those social attributes that distinguish between male and female, and are generally assumed to follow assigned sex, which is determined at birth by observation. Assigned sex is assumed to be consistent with one's biological sex.

Gender Identity Disorder

A clinical term used to describe individuals who experience a persistent anxiety, confusion or dissonance resulting from discomfort with their assigned birth sex. Other common terms are *gender confusion* or *gender dysphoria*. It manifests in a compulsive drive to dress, and actually to behave and live as members of the opposite sex (the term 'sex-role inversion' was used in the early part of the last century). Such behaviour may be for limited periods, long term, or permanent. Most people do not experience serious gender ambiguity and take their own gender identity for granted. Such a definition is not applied where a concurrent 'intersex' (*q.v.*) condition exists.

Gnosticism

The use of the historical/theological term *gnosticism* in an ethical context may be understood to refer to the tendency both to

---

2. Postulated by John Money (Emeritus Professor of Medical Psychology, Department of Psychiatry, Johns Hopkins University). Money has also expressed '... a profound belief in the biological elements of gender identity...'. See L.J.G. Gooren, M.D., Ph.D., *Body Politics: The Physical Side of Gender Identity* (New York: The Haworth Press Inc., 1991), pp.13, 16.
3. R. Holder, 'The Ethics of Transsexualism', Part 1, in *Crucible*, April–June (1998), p.90.

despise, reject, or even deny the physical creation, and additionally to claim access to a basis of knowledge that cannot effectively be tested or checked by any public criteria. Within the specific context of transsexuality, *gnosticism* may typically be manifested in the rejection or devaluation of the body, or in a desire to treat the physical as a manipulable tool to the realisation of the purposes of the supposedly 'true self'.

Gonads

Generally refers to the organs that produce the spermatozoa and ova, i.e. the testes and ovaries.

Hermaphrodite

One of a number of rare clear physiological causal medical congenital conditions where the sex of newly born babies is ambiguous due to the presence of gonads and genitalia of both sexes, such people being termed 'hermaphrodites'. An individual with *testicular feminisation syndrome*, for example, appears normal at birth, but actually has testes as well as a clitoris. The condition is usually treated in early childhood by surgery and hormone therapy.

Homosexuality/Lesbianism

The emotional and/or erotic attraction to a person of the same sex (*homosexual* – male to male; *lesbian* – female to female) and the possible acting out of that attraction. Gender confusion is usually not a significant component of homosexuality.

Intersex

Refers to a number of rare medical conditions where people are born with ambiguous sexual characteristics, and nearly always due to physiological causes. Commonly, this may be shown by the presence of intermediate forms of external genitalia. *Congenital adrenal hyperplasia*, in which a girl is born with a masculinised clitoris, and chromosomal abnormalities such as *Turner's syndrome*, are amongst the medical conditions known as 'intersex'. When an intersex condition is present there is usually a clear physiological causal condition. Male or female sex may usually (though not always) be determined by a chromosome check in such rare cases of physical ambiguity. Surgical involvement may be considered in rare cases of ambiguity. Despite frequent arguments to the contrary, transsexuality should not be regarded as a genuine recognised 'intersex' condition. Most biological investigations of transsexuals have found no abnormalities in chromosomal pattern, in the gonads (which include the internal and external sexual organs), or in sex hormone levels that could account for the condition.[4]

Sex

For working purposes this may be defined as the genetic, physical and hormonal characteristics that differentiate between male and female. Sex is usually determined at birth by observation of the physical characteristics, though in practice there may be rare ambiguities. The most basic determining factor is the chromosomal difference, with males having one 'X' and one 'Y' sex chromosome and females having two 'X' chromosomes, and the gonads. It is impossible to alter these basic factors by any surgery though rare ambiguity can occur (see *Intersex*).

Sex Reassignment Surgery (SRS)

A series of surgical (mainly plastic) operations performed to remove genitalia and alter the shape of the body to conform it more to the body of the opposite biological sex. The extent of surgery performed will vary with each individual. Public awareness of *SRS* increased dramatically after newspapers revealed that a former American G.I. had undergone such surgery under the supervision of Danish endocrinologist, Hamburger, in the early 1950s. The first such surgical operation was conducted in 1931.

---

4. L.J.G. Gooren, *The Endocrinology of Transsexualism: A Review and Commentary* (New York: Pergamon Press, 1990), p.16. Professor Gooren affirms: 'The very absence of the above-mentioned abnormalities now constitutes an element in the definition of transsexualism.'

Given that surgery cannot actually reassign *sex*, probably a more accurate term is *gender reassignment surgery (GRS)*. For comparison purposes it should also be noted that the incidence of relatively successful non-surgical adjustments in the context of psychotherapy treatment alone is in fact quite high.[5]

Transpersons

A variety of terms may be encountered in current popular usage, such as transpersons, transgendered, transmen and transwomen. Generally they are used in an attempt to legitimate what are commonly referred to as transsexuals. Transsexuals themselves often prefer to be referred to as 'transsexual men', 'transsexual women', or simply 'transsexual people'. Arguably, the use of the term transsexual could be viewed as strictly inaccurate, with the term transgendered possibly being more appropriate.

Transsexuality or Transsexualism

Transsexuality is the term used to describe the condition in which an apparently biologically normal individual feels that he or she is actually a member of the opposite sex. Medical and ethical opinion may vary as to whether there is in fact any such medical 'thing' as transsexuality. *Transsexuality* may often be marked by a strong rejection of the individual's physical sexual characteristics and, again at its most extreme, may be absolute, overwhelming and apparently unalterable. A transsexual man, for example, may feel an attraction towards other men, but unlike a homosexual will prefer to relate to them as a female. Transsexuals seek to live in their preferred gender role and may undergo surgery to conform their body to that of the opposite sex. They remain well aware of their actual anatomical sex, and for the 'condition' of transsexuality to be present no doubt will subsist concerning the actual biological sex of the individual. Psychologists see transsexuality

---

5. According to Lothstein and Levine the number is apparently as high as 70% out of 50 patients treated. As cited by Rodney Holder in *Crucible*, April–June (1998), p.94.

as the end stage of *gender identity disorder*. Some have described it in terms of a state in which the mind can no longer accept the body. Accordingly, a definition frequently encountered is that of 'feeling like a man trapped in a woman's body' or vice versa.

Transvestite/Transvestism

Transvestites have a compulsion to dress and act like members of the opposite sex, often to obtain sexual arousal. Usually they are heterosexual men, and do not exhibit any strong desire to change sex or identify themselves with members of the opposite sex, although they may spend considerable periods of time cross-dressed. In some cases, such people may, however, come to see themselves as being transsexuals and define themselves as such. Though transsexual people almost inevitably pass through a stage of transvestism, this typically may come to take the form of an identity rather than an erotic compulsion.

2

The Current and Historical Contexts

Introduction to the Present Debate

Until recently widespread ignorance about transsexuality has been customary, but with open portrayal of transsexuals on the TV screen, for example in *Coronation Street* and *Paddington Green*, and more recently by way of an *Everyman* documentary on the BBC, transsexual behaviours have recently tended to be portrayed as apparently normal variants of human sexuality. Consequently we are seeing today increasing pressure to change what are deemed to be prejudiced and inaccurate perceptions of transsexuality. Medical technology continues to offer the expectation of previously unimagined cosmetic and surgical possibilities, though consequently presenting new and controversial ethical dilemmas. Involved in these highly complex questions are implications for traditional ideas concerning what constitutes human personality, sexuality and identity. Intense debate, initiated often by interest groups representing transsexuals, includes pressing the case for reconsideration of the causes of transsexuality and the nature of

---

1. In the BBC 1 *Everyman* documentary broadcast on 24th October 1999, an Anglican parish church was apparently content to bless in church the 'marriage' of a male-to-female transsexual with a female-to-male transsexual.

sexual identity. Parliament and the legal processes are already under pressure to reflect the resultant changes in perception.

The present legal approach in the United Kingdom is to recognize sex as biologically determined, but in a rapidly changing world this nowadays appears somewhat out of line when compared with more liberal approaches adopted in some other countries which offer certain concessions to transsexuals. In Britain, post-operative transsexuals must legally retain the sex that was assigned at birth, which in practice may cause instances of difficulty or embarrassment when they seek to pursue their adopted gender in society. A key challenge for the transsexual community revolves around their legal inability to marry, an aspect of UK law that the transsexual community finds to be discriminatory, and which is not necessarily shared by other countries.[2] Though in certain quarters transsexuality has been seen as a bizarre aberration or perversion, there is now a rising climate of opinion that is being encouraged to tolerate changes in perception backed by changes in the law.

In some instances, though a code of practice does exist, it can happen that expensive plastic surgery may sometimes be offered rather too readily by medical practitioners, perhaps at the expense of research into, and treatment of the roots and causes of, the transsexual condition. There is a consequent danger of a resultant tendency towards marginalisation of associated ethical issues. Medical surgery still remains essentially highly experimental, and the proliferation of private treatment may sometimes mean that gender reassignment surgery could be resorted to before prudent investigative considerations have been thoroughly appraised, especially if a patient is urgently demanding the surgery. The outcome can be profoundly unsettling for the individual who has not been fully prepared, leading in some extreme cases to suicide.

The medical profession, interest groups, and general received public wisdom (as reflected for example in Parliamentary debate)

---

2. Notably Denmark and currently at least one state in the USA.

frequently make a common assumption that transsexuality has a biological or physiological cause (it is an 'accident of nature' or a 'genetic birth defect'), and that 'science' is close to demonstrating this, thereby increasingly opening the way for technological assistance to fit the psychology (though what is not so often mentioned is that such technology also implies the corresponding possibility of 'corrective' treatment). Others take a completely contrary view, emphasising the highly controversial, experimental and indeterminate nature of the relevant scientific research, and preferring to regard transsexuality primarily as a learned behaviour, conditioned mainly by environment, and recommending psychological treatment whilst stressing the incidence of depression, psychosis and suicide as the more extreme results of irreversible surgery. Still others believe that the cause of transsexuality is partly genetic, but mostly environmental, social and behavioural, e.g. with strong reaction against a same-sex parent during childhood, inability to bond, absent fathers, poor role modelling and abuse; all of these represent possible key influential factors.

Why Should the Church be Concerned?

Given this background what should the church's response be? It has to be acknowledged that its record on acceptance of apparently deviant and bizarre sexual expression has not been consistent. Parts of the church have gradually been influenced by cultural change to moderate their stance on, e.g. birth control, divorce, and homosexual equality. Is acceptance of transsexuality despite initial reservations similarly inevitable? On the other hand, though some church groups have evinced implacable hostility to such issues, is it right that there are in fact fundamental principles at stake requiring guidelines to be drawn now? The question cannot be ignored as many would like, particularly as special interest groups who claim self-determined gender identity as a personal right, are already demanding that the church should accept transsexual people uncritically and unconditionally.

Expertise, or indeed basic knowledge regarding transsexuality, is very scarce in the UK, especially in the Christian community. Unfortunately, because the subject is so poorly understood, when help and understanding has been sought from secular authorities or Christian sources even greater confusion has occurred. The consequences for the transsexual individuals and those seeking to care for them have sometimes been quite devastating. On the other hand, the implications for churches wishing to receive transsexual people may be far-reaching.

To date, the evangelical Christian community has not seriously attempted to respond to the issues raised by transsexuality. Where it has, it has tended to adopt differing approaches to the question: some reject the option of gender reassignment (including surgery), others cautiously approve it.[3] Though the incidence of transsexuality causing major issues within the local church context is still relatively low, requests from Christian transsexuals to participate at all levels of church life are becoming more frequent. As a consequence, complex pastoral dilemmas are increasingly being encountered. In reality, when confronted with transvestism, or if the subject of transsexuality is raised in a church, there may understandably be a mixed reaction. Some church members are likely to be quite hostile; church leaders may be quite uncertain as to how best to respond.

Some of the key complex issues that Christians need to seriously consider include:

- What determines sexual identity?
- Is it right and should it be legal for someone to change gender and dress in the clothing of the opposite sex? Is gender reassignment surgery an acceptable treatment for transsexual persons? Does the issue of gender manipulation beg the question of who plays God? Has humankind in a sense usurped the role of Creator? To what extent does gender reassignment surgery imply collusion with

---

3. See Bibliography.

falsification and illusion? Is there a need to set limitations regarding the extent to which technology should be permitted to interfere with nature? Can technology legitimately 'reassign' human identity, or are all such concerns practically and ethically irrelevant?

- Should transsexuals have a legal identity distinct from others? Should they be allowed to change birth certificates implying the consequent legal right to marry someone of the same biological sex?

- Should the Church recognise and solemnise 'marriages' or other unions of transsexual persons? Should it support the adoption and fostering of children by transsexuals? The Church's understanding of marriage is intimately involved in the debate – since for Christians only a man and a woman may marry, transsexual 'marriage' may appear a contradiction in terms. Christians generally accept there can be only two possible alternative states – monogamous heterosexual marriage or singleness and celibacy.[4] The Church is, however, increasingly under pressure to accept 'paramarital' states together with a special category of rites/ceremonies. Would such institutionalisation of transsexual marriage status represent a 'slippery slope' leading inevitably to the creation of legal public/practical pastoral doctrine contradictory to the Church's own theology?

- Should separation and divorce become a requirement? How are children likely to react?

- Should preferred gender status act as an impediment to an individual's participation in society and the community of faith?

- How should the Church respond to post-operative transsexuals and those people in the process of transition, or seeking gender reassignment surgery?

---

4. For the Evangelical Alliance position see *Faith, Hope & Homosexuality* published by the Alliance in 1998, e.g. p.32.

History of Transvestism and Transsexuality

Estimates of the incidence of *transvestism* in the general population vary from 1 to 3 per cent. The incidence of *transsexuality* is thought to be much lower.[5]

Scriptural reference to cross-dressing occurs in the book of Deuteronomy,[6] suggesting that its practice, albeit in a foreign cultic context, had been known to the Israelites even before the days of Moses. It would appear that, for some people, the drive to convincingly mimic, if not attempt to represent, the opposite sex, is not new. History records acts of cross-dressing in numerous cultures over the centuries. Frequently these practices were associated with pagan ritual worship, as was mutilation of the body. There are reports of surgical attempts to alter the physical appearance of the body in the latter part of the nineteenth century. The necessary surgical skill to alter the external characteristics of the body so that to some extent it conforms to that of the opposite sex has been developed only in the latter half of the twentieth century. Magnus Hirschfeld, the German medical scientist, introduced the term transvestism to medical literature in 1910. The lesser term 'eonism', describing a male who cross-dressed, was coined by Havelock Ellis, an English psychologist, in the 1920s after the Chevalier D'Eon, a famous eighteenth-century French courtier and transvestite.[7]

The descriptive word 'transsexual' was popularised by Harry Benjamin, an American psychiatrist, in the late 1940s and early 1950s. Transsexuality may therefore be considered to be largely a phenomenon of the late twentieth century, after the function of hormones began to be understood and surgical options became technically possible. The anguish of people who believe they are 'born into the bodies of the wrong sex' would seem to be

---

5. See p.16.
6. Deuteronomy 22:5.
7. See P. Ackroyd, *Transvestism and Drag: the History of the Obsession* (New York: Simon & Shuster, 1979).

peculiarly a product of later twentieth-century society. It is probably a consequence of a cultural milieu that promotes options and possibilities, and a moral climate that tends to relativise traditional views. Accordingly, the need to develop appropriate social responses to transsexuality is a relatively new responsibility for society and the Church at the dawn of a new millennium.

3

Medical Considerations Relating to Transsexuality

The evangelical perspective on transsexuality is adopted primarily from the witness of Scripture. Christians believe that science will ultimately, if accurate, confirm God's revealed truth if correctly understood. Scientific research requires examination, but is not of greater authority than Scripture in finding a Christian ethical basis for transsexuality.

The scientific study of transsexuality is relatively limited in scope, and apparent contradictions between scientific research and our understanding of God's revelation on the subject should, perhaps, be anticipated. In addition, if transsexuality is viewed as a contravention of 'the Maker's instructions', there is consequently likely to be less clarity, and fewer conclusions reached, in the research of a behaviour that runs contrary to God's created order. In some instances, there has been an observed tendency for selective reporting of scientific results and slanted discussion. Much of the new controversial research in this area is precisely that, 'new'. A recent research slant may be used to discover an 'original' finding and may frequently not be repeated for confirmation. Some of these 'one-off' results, at variance from other established literature, have been used quite presumptively at times as unequivocal truth by single-issue lobby groups to further agendas. They prefer spinning a story for the media to pursuing debate within the scientific forum and allowing time for further academic work. Critical discernment and understanding should, therefore, be exercised before blindly accepting what 'science' and 'medicine' apparently say about transsexuality.

The Debate Regarding Causation

Until relatively recently, the medical profession has considered transsexuality, like homosexuality, to be a pathological deviation from normal sexuality as there is no possibility of procreation. It has become customary to view transsexuality as a deviation of the social sexual differentiation process, i.e. as a *gender* issue rather than a question of *sex*. Research, until quite recently, has therefore tended to concentrate on the area of correct sexual development and the origins of gender differentiation. There is parallel, albeit indeterminate and controversial, research into the causes of homosexuality. If the outcome here were seen to favour a biological origin, then there would inevitably be added impetus to assume that transsexuality, as a cross-gender condition, owes its origins to a similar biological cause. Accordingly, recent scientific research into the causes of transsexuality has become a highly controversial area in which interest groups with specific agendas sometimes anticipate what they would like the outcome to be. For example, underlying a debate on the subject of transsexuality in the House of Commons was the assumption that the definitive cause of transsexuality had already been proven to be physiological, which, of course, fundamentally affects the way in which the condition is addressed medically, pastorally and politically.[1] In fact, research into the genetic and physiological origins of transsexuality remains inconclusive, and the likelihood is that multiple factors will be found to be involved.

---

1. See *Hansard*, 2nd February (1996), pp.1282–90.

Incidence of Transsexuality

Despite recent media interest, transsexuality is a relatively rare condition, although there is some variation in estimates of how frequent it is. About 1 in 30,000 males, and 1 in 100,000 females are estimated to be transsexual.[2] Research in the Netherlands has shown higher figures (1 in 11,900 for males, and in 1 in 30,400 for females).[3] Accordingly, the incidence of transsexuality is much less than that of homosexuality and lesbianism. Transsexuality is 300 times less common than these behaviours.[4]

Transsexual behaviour is well described in the scientific literature.[5] In males, transsexuality may begin in childhood with feelings of discomfort with bodily sexual characteristics, and occasionally with a desire to be the opposite sex. This may often lead to cross-dressing. Around puberty and afterwards this may develop into a fetish form of transvestism in which sexual arousal occurs from cross-dressing and usually culminates in masturbation. This conflict with the male gender identity may then lead to the adoption of a different gender role identity. *Transsexuality* has in effect developed, with a biological male believing that he has been somehow 'trapped in the wrong body' and should really be a woman. The development of transsexuality is different in females where the fetish element (of being sexually aroused by a symbol,

---

2. T. Gallarda, I. Amado, S. Coussinoux, M.F. Poirier, B. Cordier and J.P. Olie, 'The Transsexualism Syndrome: Clinical Aspects and Therapeutic Prospects' in *Encephale*, 1997, No.23, pp.321–26; S.L. Bem, *The Lenses of Gender* (New Haven, Connecticut: Yale University Press, 1993).

3. P.J.M. Van Kesteren, L.J. Gooren and J.A. Megens, 'An epidemiological and demographic study of transsexuals in the Netherlands' in *Archives of Sexual Behaviour* 25 (1996) pp.13–26. Cultural factors in the Netherlands mean that transvestism tends not to be recognised as a separate 'condition', and is equated more with transsexuality, in contrast to the UK.

4. N.E. Whitehead and B.K. Whitehead, *My Genes Made Me Do It!* (Lafayette, Louisiana: Huntington House 1999).

5. J. Bancroft, 'Sexual Disorders' in R.E. Kendell and A.K. Zealley (eds), *Companion to Psychiatric Studies* (Edinburgh: Churchill Livingstone, 1987), pp.620–22.

i.e. clothing of the opposite sex) is less important, if not absent. In both sexes though, there is an obsessive striving to change appearance and behaviour to mimic that of the opposite sex.

We may conveniently condense the scientific debate into three main questions:

- Are transsexual people born that way?
- Is the best way to help a transsexual the provision of radical treatments which make the subject look and behave more like their desired (opposite) sex?
- Is transsexuality inevitable?

Are Transsexual People Born That Way?

Different explanations for the development of transsexuality have been offered. Some have suggested that it is due either to an abnormal gene, altered levels of hormones in the body, or because some part of the body (often the brain) is more like the opposite sex in the way it works. Others have suggested that these physical causes are not important, and rather than transsexual people being born with their sexual identity pre-set, influences in the person's environment, such as an abusive father or an emotionally cold mother, are more likely causes which give rise to feelings of rejection of the body and a life of denial with regard to one's biological sex. Some argue that these psychological causes (which research has consistently confirmed for several decades) may combine with physical ones (published research here is comparatively recent) to produce transsexuality. In this '*nature* versus *nurture*' debate Christians are frequently drawn to the *nurture* or environmental arguments; it seems 'impossible' to conceive that God could create somebody with a predetermined wish to change sex, having been born into the 'wrong' type of body. For opposite reasons, using the *nature* argument, groups in favour of gender reassignment have argued that transsexual people have no choice about their desires, and that it is psychologically impossible for them to have their wish to change sex modified, i.e. it is a physiological or medical 'condition'.

Various studies have been utilised to suggest that transsexuality is a condition that is enforced because of biological aetiology, but the findings are not conclusive. A suggestion that transsexual people possess different sexual hormone levels[6] from heterosexuals has not been scientifically reproduced. There is an anecdotal report of protein circulating in the blood of female-to-male transsexuals that is related to the Y-chromosome (the chromosome found only in males), but this proved irreproducible by others and even by the original team.[7] Research has more convincingly shown that female-to-male transsexuals are more masculine than the average female in body build.[8] In a small sample of female-to-male transsexuals a significant proportion (6/16), had an overactive adrenal gland (a body organ that produces male-like hormones and can therefore make a woman's body appear more masculine). In these cases, the perception of the women by themselves, and by others, of being 'less feminine' may well have predisposed them to develop in a transsexual direction. It remains unclear how such a pathway might operate in practice, but it could be mediated through psychological factors, for example as a result of the women being treated in a more masculine way by third parties, or from poor self-esteem resulting from a feeling of difference. However, many argue that physical differences such as these indicate that transsexual people have been born 'different', and their physical appearance indicates that there are other

---

6. H.A.G. Bosinski, M. Peter, G. Bonatz, R. Arndt, M. Heidenreich, N.G. Siffell and R. Wille, 'A Higher Rate of Hyperandrogenic Disorders in Female to Male Transsexuals' in *Psychoneuroendocrinology* 22 (1997), pp.361–80.

7. K.J. Zucker and S.J. Bradley, *Gender Identity Disorder and Psychosexual Problems in Children and Adolescents* (New York: Guildford Press, 1995).

8. H.A.G. Bosinski, I. Schroder, M. Peter, R. Arndt, R. Wille and W.G. Sippell, 'Anthropometrical Measurements and Androgen Levels in Males, Females and Hormonally Untreated Female-to-Male Transsexuals', *Archives of Sexual Behaviour* 26 (1997), pp.143–57.

physiological differences, such as brain structure and function. Whilst the 'cause and effect' argument is not clear, certainly the psychological explanation suggested above appears more obvious and straightforward.

Despite media interest focusing on them, the strength of studies that claim transsexual people have a different brain structure is very limited. The allegation of supposed biological differences has been used to argue that transsexual behaviour is a result of innate, physical factors that are not chosen by the individual. Claims made by Dutch authors[9] that a specific part of the brain (the bed nucleus of the *stria terminalis*) is female-sized in male-to-female transsexuals are based on studies of the post-mortem brains of transsexuals who were prescribed hormones of the opposite sex. But the differences found in these brains may have been caused by the hormonal medications, and may not have been present prior to the chemical manipulation. In addition, as is well known, the structure of the brain can alter after new experiences and behaviours,[10] and these brain structures may well have altered as a result of the specific behaviours adopted by the subjects. As such, the differences in brain structure may have been an *effect* of transsexuality rather than its cause. Post-mortem brain studies are notoriously difficult to perform and unreliable. It is unlikely that any similar research will ever be able to show differences in the brain structures of transsexuals that clearly evidence causality.

With such interest in attempting to show a physiological cause for transsexuality some have alternatively postulated a genetic cause for the condition. In the event that people are born 'transsexual' it is theoretically possible that the cause could be as a result of abnormal genetic material. However, no research has

---

9. J.N. Zhou, M.A. Hofman, L.J.G. Gooren and D.F. Swaab, 'A Sex Difference in the Human Brain and its Relation to Transsexuality', *Nature* 378 (1995), pp.68–70.

10. E.R. Kandel and R.D. Hawkins, 'The Biological Basis of Learning and Individuality' in *Scientific American* 267(3) (1992), pp.53–60.

been able to demonstrate the existence of such a 'transsexual gene'.[11]

The arguments set out above do lack a corrective perspective on the debate, which may be supplied by other important related areas, notably those stressing the link between behaviour and genetics. Research has shown that behaviours such as alcoholism[12] and criminality[13] do have a genetic link and appear to be inherited. Even if a genetic link to transsexuality were to be proved (which it definitively has not), it would effectively be suggesting to a transsexual person, 'You were born that way, you can't change and you don't need to.' This could be analogous to telling an alcoholic, 'It's all in your genes, have another drink!' Some people may find this type of analogy somewhat offensive, but the point at issue is that genetics should not be used as a blanket argument to remove moral choice-making and responsibility from individuals. To do otherwise is to dehumanise and diminish respect for human beings. Very few scientists would accept that any given organism's actions are 'fated' and beyond their control. In the debate on homosexuality, some pro-gay sex groups and researchers have notably moved away from arguing that genes and brain chemicals are the cause of sexual orientation;[14] they are no doubt concerned that somebody will suggest that, if a chemical imbalance

---

11. In this connection, if transsexuality were to be a purely genetic condition, it could be expected, for example, that in the case of identical twins (who have exactly the same genes), if one was transsexual then the other would be also. This, however, has not been demonstrated by any known research. See N. Buhrich, J.M. Bailey and N.G. Martin, 'Sexual Orientation, Sexual Identity, and Sex-Dimorphic Behaviors in Male Twins' in *Behaviour Genetics* 21 (1991), pp.75–96; G.M.F. Garden and D.J. Rothery, 'A Female Monozygotic Twin Pair Discordant for Transsexualism – Some Theoretical Implications' in *British Journal of Psychiatry* 161 (1992), pp.852–54.

12. C.R. Cloninger, M. Bohman and S. Sigvardsson, 'Inheritance of Alcohol Abuse', *Archives of General Psychiatry* 38 (1981), p.861.

13. K.O. Christiansen, 'The Genesis of Aggressive Criminality' in J. de Wit and W.W. Hartup (eds), *Determinants of the Origins of Aggressive Behaviour* (The Hague: Mouton, 1974), pp.233–53.

14. See, for example, N. G. Messer, *Genes, Persons and God* (Grove Ethical Studies No.95, Nottingham, 1994), p.7 or *Christianity Today*, 4th October 1999, p.53.

is found in those who are sexually deviant, they should be given corrective medical treatment (e.g. by tablets) to change. Transsexual lobby groups may undergo a similar change of opinion.

Although it may be surprising to many, there is controversy in the debate on physical causes of transsexuality as to how 'sex' is defined, i.e. what makes a person male or female. In the overwhelming majority of individuals (99.5%) sex, if defined by physical characteristics (the presence of a vagina or a penis), is obvious at birth. In a very small number of children, as a result of one of a number of known medical conditions (such as *adrenal virilisation syndrome*, in which girls are born with a masculinised clitoris), their genitalia may be ambiguous, and it may actually be unclear what sex they are.[15] In the case of *testicular feminisation syndrome*, a healthy-looking baby may be born as an apparent girl, and may pass through puberty initially in a normal way, but nevertheless does not proceed to commence periods (the child cannot do so as it has testes inside its abdomen rather than a womb and ovaries). Analysing a blood sample is a possible aid to specifying the true sex of such individuals as it may identify their chromosomes. Males have the sex chromosomes XY; females XX. However, in the case of *testicular feminisation syndrome*, for example, in which the individual possesses the male chromosomes XY together with the external body of a female, it would normally be regarded as preferable to raise that child as a woman. Chromosome analysis may also present problems when extremely rare results such as XO (*Turner's syndrome*) or XXY (*Klinefelter's syndrome*) are discovered. However, if a Y chromosome is present the person is generally defined as being of male sex. Usual medical practice is to raise a child in the sex that they are physically (not chromosomally) most similar to, and this appears a compassionate and sensible approach. These examples, although they are dealing with known medical abnormalities, do show that defining 'sex' from a scientific point of view (by external genitalia, internal genitalia or chromosomes) can in practice be less than straightforward.

---

15. J. Money and A.A. Ehrhardt, *Man & Woman, Boy & Girl* (Baltimore: The Johns Hopkins University Press, 1972).

Hermaphroditism is a very rare condition, one cause being *testicular feminisation syndrome*, in which both male and female sexual organs are present (with this disorder, a clitoris and testes). However, there is no comparison here with the case of transsexuality. The sexual organs of transsexuals are physically and functionally normal. By definition, a transsexual person believes he or she is trapped in the wrong type of physical body and desires their sexual organs changed to that of the opposite sex. Transsexuality on this basis is clearly, therefore, a psychological not a physical 'condition'. Despite this, some have argued that all transsexuals are indeed hermaphrodites. There is, however, no physical evidence whatsoever for this. One authority in the field has advanced the argument that transsexuals have an 'intersex' condition of the brain.[16] An 'intersex' condition, however, exists when the techniques for identifying sex are inconclusive due to ambiguity of the genitalia, and not because of brain characteristics. Accordingly, on the usual understandings, transsexuals do not have an 'intersex' condition. Moreover, as previously discussed, any evidence of a pre-existing difference in brain structure or function in transsexuals is lacking. To suggest, then, that transsexual people have some physical parts of the opposite sex is incorrect and quite misleading.

Gender reassignment surgery by definition acknowledges primacy to psychological perception over physical evidence; however, the body of evidence for transsexuality having a *psychological* cause is significantly greater and long-standing in contrast to the *biological* research.[17] Experts cited by transsexual groups have

---

16. L.J.G. Gooren, 'Closing speech: The Council of Europe: 23rd Colloquy on European Law' in *Transsexualism, Medicine and Law* (Strasbourg: Council of Europe, 1995).

17. Rodney Holder draws attention to the 'biological' versus 'psychological' debate in his article in *Crucible*, April–June, 1998, p.92. He rightly raises concerns that are becoming increasingly important with regard to the implications of, e.g. prenatal biological causation for DNA testing and potential foetus abortion. Though the implications of psychological aetiology for moral responsibility and appropriate treatment are also stressed.

suggested that, 'transsexualism could be a body image disorder rather than being an expression of a pseudohermaphroditic development'.[18] Published academic literature that indicates that transsexual people as children have experienced much greater psychological harm than non-transsexuals remains largely undisputed. Typical associated damage has included, for example, suffering the effects of parents who were rejecting,[19] or who themselves suffered from a mental illness.[20] In many cases of extreme gender dysphoria, the father was physically absent during childhood. Many transsexuals report an emotionally distant father. Despite the undisputed quality of this long-standing research, ironically there has been little recent media focus on it. It seems that some pro-transsexual lobby groups have preferred to emphasise physical causes, notwithstanding that some are completely unfounded, perhaps fearing a response that psychological causes imply the possibility of psychological treatment or therapy. Of course, if physical causation was to be demonstrated, the same argument with regard to potential corrective physical or genetic treatment would apply. One line of argument suggests that there may be slight physical differences in children, which apparently cause parents to treat their children differently. Although this does warrant serious investigation, it is difficult to accept too seriously that minor physical differences or unusual gender-related behaviour could be the sole or major cause of frequent parental

---

18. Professor Louis Gooren (Professor of Transsexology at the Free University Hospital, Amsterdam), along with Professor John Money (Associate Professor of Medical Psychology, Department of Psychiatry, Johns Hopkins University). See L.J.G. Gooren, 'Concepts and Methods of Biomedical Research into Homosexuality and Transsexualism', *Journal of Psychology & Human Sexuality* 6(1) (1993), p.14.
19. P.T. Cohen-Kettenis and W.A. Arrindell, 'Perceived Parental Rearing Style, Parental Divorce and Transsexualism: a Controlled Study', *Psychological Medicine* 20 (1990), pp.613–20.
20. G.A. Rekers, 'Gender Identity Disorder' in G.A. Rekers, J.S. Oakes and J. Gray (eds), *The Journal of Human Sexuality* (Carrollton, Texas: Lewis & Stanley, 1996), pp.11–20.

rejection, or account for the anecdotal reports of greatly increased rates in transsexuals of sexual abuse as children.

Is Radical Drug and Surgical Treatment the Best Way to Help a Transsexual?

Most Christians would probably respond to the suggestion of gender reassignment surgery in the negative. Transsexual people tend usually to choose to dress in the clothes of the opposite gender, either occasionally (as with transvestites), or permanently. By using hormone tablets (or occasionally injections) body size and shape can be altered. Men who take female hormones (most commonly oestrogen) will develop physical features including breasts and a feminine shaped pelvis. Women who take male hormones (such as testosterone) will develop a deeper voice, increased muscle mass and facial hair. Treatment may be continued by breast reduction (in women) or augmentation (in men). Men may use speech therapy and facial hair removal to increase their feminine appearance. The final irrevocable step for both sexes is genital change. A more convincing image may be fashioned by gender reassignment surgery in men than in women. Most transsexuals who undergo gender reassignment surgery are relatively satisfied and adapt reasonably well (at least in the medium term),[21] frequently presenting a very realistic impersonation of the opposite sex. For many it is 'a dream come true'. Indeed, many who undergo gender reassignment report a shift or increase in sexual attraction that complements their new physical appearance. Suspicions are rightly raised that transsexuals will naturally be reluctant to voice regrets over their choice. Though gender reassignment

---

21. O. Bodlund and G. Kullgren, 'Transsexualism – General Outcome and Prognostic Factors: A Five Year Follow-up Study of Nineteen Transsexuals in the Process of Changing Sex', *Archives of Sexual Behaviour* 25 (1996), pp.303–16.

surgery is largely irreversible, at least a small number later do regret their decision,[22] and a few even readopt their former heterosexual lifestyle. For some the surgery is undoubtedly a disastrous error.[23] The investment a person makes in gender reassignment financially, emotionally and physically is enormous; it is an expensive one-way ticket.

Christians believe that personal happiness and fulfilment are found through pleasing God and obedience to his revealed will. The adoption of a theological position that regards an individual's sex as a 'given' from God implies that radical modern plastic surgery, notwithstanding that it may offer what many transsexual people desire, represents a distortion of God's creation. Of course, a problem with this line of argument concerns where we draw the line, and most Christians do happily accept many forms of cosmetic surgery. Nevertheless, change is not impossible. In a recent documented case study, a man who became a Christian after undergoing gender reassignment surgery became convinced that he was effectively living an illusion in his assumed feminine role and needed to revert to his true masculine identity. Subsequently, his sexual desire has once more become re-directed to women.[24] Such a decision to revert would have been made at considerable cost, in part due to the insurmountable difficulties in reversing the surgical changes. This problem inevitably has to be faced by all those who have undergone gender reassignment surgery and who subsequently decide to revert their gender, particularly for men, since there is as yet comparatively little surgical experience in this area.

Despite gender reassignment surgery meeting many of the wishes of transsexual people and affording a measure of increased

---

22. M. Landen, J. Wallinder, G. Hambert and B. Lundstrom, 'Factors Predictive of Regret in Sex Reassignment', *Acta Pscyhiatrica Scandinavica* 97 (1998), pp.284–89.
23. As acknowledged by *The Lancet*. See Rodney Holder in *Crucible*, April–June, 1998, p.94.
24. *Overcoming Transsexuality: A Christian Testimony* (Watford: Parakaleo Ministry 1999).

comfort (at least in the short term), it nevertheless cannot pretend to treat root psychological causes similar to those which are responsible for people rejecting their bodies. These include peer pressure, perfectionism, media images, parental and self-rejection and the consequent poor self-esteem, which of course may unfortunately be reinforced by hostile reception in society. Gender reassignment surgery has often been resorted to from the limited perspective of prioritising the patient's wish to change gender, and in consequence minimises recognition of the hurts and traumas that in all likelihood have caused the condition in the first place. Though proponents may argue that gender reassignment is an act of mercy and compassion, and may point to statistics that allege a degree of success, nevertheless long-term statistics are lacking, and the surgery may equally be viewed as offering fleeting and false comfort to a hurting individual. In many instances it does not lead to long-term relief from the root causes of gender dysphoria. In this context, it should be acknowledged that there are essentially two distinctive ways of viewing the 'treatment' of transsexuality: is it 'tackling the illness' or 'managing the symptoms'? These depend on what account of sexual identity is adopted and will, in turn, lead to different accounts of surgical intervention for transsexuals. It will have become apparent that this report considers surgical intervention largely to be 'managing the symptoms'.

Transsexuality can be seen as a form of addiction. Initial habitual cross-dressing can lead, in due course, to the all-consuming desire to change gender as a result of compulsive behaviour. To recommend gender reassignment surgery as 'the solution' may consequently be viewed as unhelpful encouragement to submit to the distorted image of self. It is a solution that allows the deep psychological confusion and hurt suffered by transsexual people to go untreated, thereby increasing the prospect of future emotional damage. Rather than allowing this to occur, the Church should be able to offer a fuller hope. A Christian response that emphasises both psychological and physical wholeness, rather than concentrating exclusively on artificial and cosmetic physical changes in the hope that they will of themselves produce the desired psychosomatic unity, more truly reflects a biblical view of holistic health.[25]

Is Transsexuality Inevitable?

The answer to the question 'can transsexuals be helped to resolve the associated issues without inevitable compulsion to resort to the label and lifestyle of transsexuality?' is not in doubt – transsexuals can and do change their gender identity and preference. In some cases, transsexual behaviour has ceased when a concurrent psychiatric condition has been treated with medication. In one documented case, a man treated for obsessive-compulsive disorder had both this condition and transsexuality remit.[26] In another case, a patient with schizophrenia developed a transsexual condition. Improvements in the schizophrenia were paralleled by a decrease in transsexual behaviour. It is possible the patient's false belief of being in the wrong body may have had origins in the abnormal thought processes of the associated schizophrenia rather than in a simple diagnosis of transsexuality. In the case cited previously,[27] a man who had previously undergone gender reassignment surgery reverted to his original gender. He subsequently married, enjoys a heterosexual lifestyle, and attributes his change to God-given help. As yet there exists no published collection of such cases in which change appears to have resulted out of choice, but other anecdotal accounts do exist.[28] Of course,

---

25. Of course there is a major distinction between *medically indicated* cosmetic surgery (e.g. where a disfigurement or deformity needs to be corrected), and purely *optional* cosmetic surgery (e.g. to change the disliked shape of one's nose).
26. I.M. Marks and D. Mataix-Cols, 'Four Year Remission of Transsexualism After Comorbid Obsessive-Compulsive Disorder Improved with Self-exposure Therapy', a case report: *British Journal of Psychiatry* 171 (1997), pp.389–90.
27. *Transsexualism in the Church: A Pastor Responds* (Watford: Parakaleo Ministry, 1998).
28. N.E. Whitehead, *Should Transsexuality be Freely Endorsed by Christians?* (Lower Hutt, New Zealand: 1999).

there are also anecdotal accounts where transsexual people claim divine support in the adoption of a transsexual lifestyle. However, it is clear there is capacity for reversal, and a number of transsexuals do revert. This represents further evidence that transsexuality is not a pre-set immutable 'condition'.

Transsexuality represents a small, specialised subject, concerning which there is still a general lack of good replicated research (not including the psychological arena in which there is relatively little controversy). Some recent research on the possible physical causes of transsexuality has been utilised as ammunition to legitimise transsexual lobby groups' agendas. Substantive debate on whether transsexual feelings are determined from birth continues, but the evidence for this is not compelling. We remain convinced that re-adoption of original gender roles, though difficult, is certainly possible for some transsexuals.

4

Political and Legal Considerations Relating to Transsexuality

Since transsexuality has become an interest group issue, questions and motions relating to transsexuality are now common in the Houses of Parliament. In February 1996 a private member's bill was introduced to the Commons[1] aimed at allowing transsexuals to obtain new birth certificates, enjoy employment protection, marry, and adopt children. Although this bill stood no chance of progress, the then Health Minister indicated that the Government were proposing to look at the whole issue. This was confirmed on 14th April 1999 when the new Labour Home Secretary announced the setting up of an inter-departmental working group to consider the particular issue of the status of transsexuals. The group was due to report by Easter 2000.[2] Its terms of reference were:

To consider, with particular reference to birth certificates, the need for appropriate legal measures to address the problems experienced by transsexuals, having due regard to scientific and societal developments, and measures undertaken in other countries to deal with this issue.

---

1. The *Gender Identity (Registration and Civil Status) Bill; Hansard,* 2nd February (1996), pp.1282–90.
2. Now published by the Home Office as 'Report of the Interdepartmental Working Group on Transsexual People'.

The setting up of the working group came in direct response to a mandate from the European Court of Human Rights which in 1998 had reprimanded the UK Government for its failure to keep under review the 'need for appropriate measures' in this area, and the government thus had little choice but to respond.

It has become important for Christians to take account of the implications of UK law as it relates to sex discrimination and homosexuality. Similar responsibilities of awareness exist with transsexuality. The most important legal issues concerned with transsexuality can be divided into three main categories. First, there are questions relating to gender reassignment surgery. Second, there are matters of personal identity and its consequences, including the current debate relating to birth certificates. Finally, there is the issue of discrimination against transsexuals. It is proposed to review each of these areas in turn, inevitably involving some considerable detail.

Transsexuality and Gender Reassignment Surgery

1. *The Legality of Gender Reassignment Surgery*

The issue of the legality of such surgery has never been specifically addressed in English law. Court decisions about the identity and rights of post-operative transsexuals have failed even to raise the question of whether the operations themselves may be carried out. There is thus a presumption that they do not infringe the civil and criminal laws against causing bodily harm. The principle of respect for individual autonomy goes some way towards legitimising procedures (even injurious ones) done with the consent of the subject. For example, it permits dangerous contact sports, but not acts that are purely designed to harm and have no intrinsic merit, such as duelling or sadomasochistic activities. Many would treat gender reassignment surgery in the same way as 'cosmetic' operations. The procedure is done on holistic grounds with the intention of improving self-esteem; the destruction of one part leads to the enhancement of the whole person.

Of course, in order for this rationale to be applied, it is necessary for the surgeon to be convinced that there *will* in fact be this enhancement of general well-being. In legal terms, surgeons might well be held negligent (or even face criminal liability) if they did not first require the sort of rigorous assessment, which is carried out in reputable gender identity clinics (often referred to as 'the real life test').

A somewhat different rationale for gender reassignment surgery has found favour in some recent UK decisions[3] in which the courts noted that transsexuality was a 'recognised gender identity dysphoria', and agreed to the inclusion of gender identity dysphoria within the *DSM IV* (*Diagnostic and Statistical Manual, 4th edition*), the American Psychiatric Association's widely cited manual of psychiatric classification. Accordingly, it was felt that gender reassignment was *not* to be likened to a mere cosmetic operation, but rather was a *physical* treatment of a *psychological* illness.

Although the *DSM* is a well-respected system of classification it is, to some extent, culturally relative. There are also a number of confusing contradictions inherent in its approach to transsexuality that need to be thought through in more detail and not ignored, as they often are. Many transsexuals would not appreciate being described as in need of treatment for a mental illness. Indeed, the presence of a mental illness would normally preclude surgery in most reputable centres where potential recipients of these harrowing operations are expected to be relatively emotionally mature and psychologically stable. But the courts can only justify treatment by surgical invasion when they identify a *mental* illness. Yet, as we have already noted, the majority of transsexual patients do not regard their problem as a psychological one; they see it as essentially a physical one. Ironically, it is this conviction that affords the necessary grounds for the courts to think that a transsexual person could be mentally ill!

---

3. *S-T (formerly J)* v *J* [1998] 1 All ER 431 and *R* v *N.W. Lancashire Health Authority, ex parte A, B and C*, Queen's Bench Division, 21st December 1998 (unreported).

What is also puzzling in this scenario is the absence of clear input from the practioners themselves. They believe transsexual patients have a 'special kind' of mental illness, rather than a 'typical' one, and it is this that qualifies them for surgery. But what does '"special kind" of mental illness' mean? What is actually wrong with the patient? These questions have yet to be satisfactorily answered.

2. *Publicly Funded Gender Reassignment Surgery*

A limited amount of public provision of gender reassignment surgery is currently available under the NHS. Most of this is carried out in a few specialist centres. Health Authorities in which these are situated must decide on the funding to be allocated to them; other authorities have the option of sending prospective patients to a centre outside their area via an 'extra-contractual referral'. A number of leading legal cases have established that resource allocation decisions are delicate balancing exercises and essentially are to be left to the authorities in question unless a decision taken is clearly unreasonable. However, policies must be clear and defensible. The North West Lancashire Health Authority took the decision not to fund extra-contractual referrals for gender reassignment surgery unless there were 'exceptional circumstances over and above clinical need'. The authority said it *would* fund psychotherapy aimed at helping transsexuals accept their biological gender. A group of three transsexuals successfully challenged this policy in a 1998 legal case.[4] They succeeded in part because the authority could not come up with any 'exceptional circumstances', which might fulfil the condition it stipulated, thus rendering it meaningless and misleading. The court reviewing the case also took the view that, although a health authority might decide it did not have the resources to fund gender reassignment surgery, it could not take a clinical view that such surgery was not, in some cases, an appropriate

---

4. Ibid.

treatment of the 'illness' gender identity dysphoria when medical opinion was to the contrary.

Despite this court ruling, health authorities may well continue to give gender reassignment surgery low priority in their funding decisions (as they do other non-life-saving procedures). Some years ago, one urologist writing in the *British Medical Journal* questioned the wisdom of his own hospital's support of this surgery when he described how many other urgent urological operations he could perform for the price of one person's gender reassignment.[5] There seems little likelihood of a central mandate to give top priority to cases of gender reassignment in a financially stretched NHS.

3. 'On-Demand' Gender Reassignment Surgery

It is an accepted fact in medical law that no patient can 'demand' of a doctor any form of medical treatment simply because he or she thinks it necessary. This is in part related to the above-mentioned issue of resource allocation. More importantly, it is because doctors are not legally permitted to provide treatment unless they are of the view that it is appropriate to do so and in the best interests of their patient. To act otherwise would be to incur charges of battery, especially if things went wrong.

Of course, if a treatment is medically indicated, then the doctor may be legally responsible for not providing it, or for failing to refer the patient to someone else more expert in the relevant area. The law supports the views of the 'reasonable' doctor. If most members of the medical profession think that a person presenting with gender identity dysphoria is in need of specialist attention, then it would be wrong for a doctor not to seek this. However, it is certainly not the view of the specialists in this field that surgery is indicated in every case in which it is requested. Experts are highly selective in deciding who will be

---

5. G. Williams, 'Gender Reassignment Today', *British Medical Journal* 295 (1987), p.671.

given the surgery. This is quite appropriate, given its gravity and irreversibility. For these reasons, it is highly unlikely that any official steps towards securing 'surgery on demand' would ever be taken.

Transsexuality and Personal Identity

Despite repeated challenges, English law has remained essentially unchanged since the leading case of *Corbett* v *Corbett* in 1972.[6] That case essentially preferred a 'biological' to a 'psychological' definition of gender and ruled that a person who was chromosomally male and who had been born with male gonads and genitals was, in law, a man, whatever surgery and hormonal treatment had later brought about.

1. *Birth Certificates*

British transsexuals are already permitted to alter most forms of identification documents in line with their 'new' gender. For example, the 'Mr', etc. identifiers can be omitted from the passport and driving licence, the two forms of identification most commonly used. However, both domestic and European courts have consistently refused to allow transsexuals' birth certificates to be altered.[7] It has been held that the birth certificate is a statement of historical fact and could not be altered if the original facts were correctly stated.[8] The European Court of Human Rights has consistently refused to overturn the UK's

---

6. *Corbett v Corbett (Otherwise Ashley)* [1971] P 83 (followed in *R v Tan and others* [1983] 1 QB 1083).
7. *Re P and G (Transsexuals)* [1996] 2 Fam Law Rep 90; *Sheffield and Horsham, Cossey, Rees* above, notes 1, 2, 3.
8. Although this has not been formally tested in the courts, there has, however, been a suggestion of allowing some leeway in the case of a person born with a biological 'intersex' condition to be re-registered; but since the only recorded case has arguably been one of historical *error,* it may not be relevant to our present concerns. See p.58.

domestic policy, stating that no new scientific evidence has been presented to change the court's original position, and that there was not sufficiently coherent weight of agreement among European member states to conclude that the UK policy infringed the basic rights of transsexuals. However, the Court did order the government to keep the matter under review, as noted above.

It is important to note that the European Court of Human Rights has taken a different view of the identity cards used in many other European countries. For example, it was decided that a French identity card was fundamentally different from a UK birth certificate.[9] First, it provided an ongoing record of civil status and incorporated various life changes such as marriage. Second, it was far more likely to be required on a day-to-day basis, thus causing frequent distress for the transsexual person who would have to explain the discrepancy between his/her appearance and the official sex on the document. In line with this ruling, a number of European states now allow the identity card to note the new gender. Some impose conditions (e.g. this change can only be made post-operatively, with a certificate from the surgeon that the individual is no longer capable of procreation in his/her original sex role). There are also some jurisdictions in which transsexuals may have their official documents altered, but this change is not sufficient to give them the capacity to enter fully into the role of the new gender, e.g. to marry.

Given the possibility of curtailing the consequences of such a change (particularly capacity to marry), the alteration of the birth certificate *in itself* may not be of particular harm to the fabric of society. We allow certain forms of amendment to the original documents in the certificates issued to adopted persons. And we do not consider it essential in every case for the birth certificate to be a perfect record of biological truth. For example, children born as the result of donor insemination are recorded as being

---

9. *B* v *France* [1992] 2 Fam Law Rep 249.

the children of their social, not their biological fathers. The potential harm caused to society or its members would probably be fairly limited, in contrast with the relief transsexuals would experience. Nevertheless, some may be concerned that to sanction the alteration of birth certificates might seem an official collusion in deception (the manner in which the amendment was carried out might go some way towards addressing this concern). Others look beyond the significance of the document itself and are worried about the possibility of further implications – the 'slippery slope' argument. We will consider some of the implications of birth certificate alteration in the next section.

2. Marriage

For many transsexuals, the impetus behind a legal change of sex is their desire to marry as a member of the new sex. English law limits marriage to that between a man and a woman (biologically defined). Purported marriages between members of the same sex are void (as, for example, are bigamous marriages). A 'void' marriage can be challenged by anyone. By contrast, a 'voidable' marriage can be challenged only by one of the spouses on grounds such as fraud or non-consummation. If the spouses are both happy with the situation, the marriage remains valid. If either a void or a voidable marriage is successfully challenged, a decree of nullity results. The petitioner does not need to seek a divorce and the marriage is treated for most purposes in law as if it had never existed.

Legally, many of the benefits conferred automatically by marriage can also be arranged between two people without the status of marriage. For example, wills can be made in favour of the other, property purchased in both names and agreements drawn up to deal with the possibility of a later separation. The marriage covenant remains a unique, solemn and public declaration of commitment and seems to retain a special role, even for many of those who give it no religious significance or who have personal experience of the ever-increasing divorce rate. Many of those in much less traditional relationships (e.g. homosexual and transsexual people who want so deeply to be treated as full members of the gender their chromosomes and biological history belie) share society's attraction to marriage.

Are there good reasons for continuing to deny state marriage to such people? Certainly, there are features of typical marriages that would not be present in a transsexual marriage. Inability to procreate would be a necessary feature of such a marriage, but many infertile couples in heterosexual marriages share this. Particularly analogous are those who marry in the knowledge that this aspect of the relationship will not be open to them. In the transsexual situation, there is the additional problem of inability to consummate the marriage, especially in the case of the female-to-male transsexual.[10] However, whilst non-consummation has always been a ground of nullity, such marriages are only voidable at the behest of the other party; presumably there would be resistance to the idea of denying the possibility of marriage outright to those who through disease or accident were unable to consummate the marriage, as long as the prospective spouse was aware of the situation.

Same-sex marriage very openly challenges our traditional assumptions about the partners in a married relationship. Transsexual marriage would do so covertly. Would it be destructive of the unique nature of marriage for us to know that a transsexual who looked like and acted like a woman and who felt herself to be a woman was allowed to marry a man? This is a difficult question that presents several complex aspects. For example, what makes it particularly difficult are situations similar to that encountered in one legal case involving a male-to-female transsexual.[11] This person now saw himself/herself as a lesbian woman. She met a female partner and legally married her (because 'she' was of course biologically male). This situation seems at

---

10. Although rather surprisingly there are a number of instances of women who believed they were married to men during long years of life with a female-to-male transsexual. For example, *Re J, minors* 2nd October 1997 (unreported); *S-T (formerly J) v J*, above, note 4.

11. *Chessington v Reed* [1998] ICR 97.

least as much an affront to the state's purpose for marriage as the silent affront posed by two partners who at least *appear* to the world to be male and female despite the underlying element of deception.[12]

Presumably, both the question of birth certificates and that of capacity to marry will come under consideration as part of this government's review of the law. As mentioned earlier, they are not necessarily linked; amendment of a birth certificate need not necessarily lead to the entitlement to marry. There are two legal issues that need to be resolved in either case. The first is a threshold question. If a change in status is to be permitted, what are its preconditions? If we are being asked to redefine the meanings of 'man' and 'woman' then which definition are we to select? A legal definition must be precise enough to cover the whole range of issues relating to gender identity, especially if we are still, for example, to prohibit same-sex marriage.

A difficulty with transsexuality is that it is largely concerned with a state of mind – a person's desires and psychological identification – rather than any concrete set of facts. Some transsexuals simply feel they are members of the opposite sex; others have begun to live their lives in this role. Many have hormone treatments to effect secondary sex characteristics and some go on to have surgery, whether to remove bodily features of their former gender or to construct those pertaining to the new gender. Should all, or only some of these be permitted to change gender legally? Allowing gender to be a matter of choice is one possibility. It would be consistent with a world-view in which self-determination is an important value. However, it would lack certainty and predictability and would be open to manipulation by anyone for whom it might be in some way advantageous to

---

12. In a recent case highlighted in the *Daily Mail* on 24th March 2000, Diane Maddox, a divorced male-to-female transsexual, who is also father to a daughter, was legally married to a lesbian woman, Clair Ward-Jackson, in an overt 'lesbian' relationship. It is worthy of note that although keen to persuade society to accept her in her new gender role, she did not consider it incongruous to make use of her biological sex for the purposes of manipulating the law.

be temporarily 'male' or 'female' for certain purposes – if only by same-sex couples wishing to evade the rules about marriage. The alternative is to presume gender to be as recorded in the original birth certificate unless a person could provide some evidence of a change of situation. But what evidence and what would it really add? We could require evidence of hormone treatments, but they are reversible. We could require evidence of surgery. That offers more in the way of certainty, but to make it the focal point would be to suggest that the removal of certain body parts actually changes a person's gender. As one court put it, although by surgery a person may have lost certain characteristics of his original sex, he has not thereby acquired those of the opposite sex.[13] It cannot actually create a new sex. There is also something faintly distasteful about requiring a sort of mutilating operation with infertility implications to take place before an individual is granted what they want, especially given that we clearly acknowledge the desire (the psychological identification) to be the critical factor in allowing a change.

The second major legal problem in allowing legal change of sex relates specifically to the marriage issue. It is the question of fraud. We might choose to allow transsexuals to marry once their birth certificates record the new sex, but it would seem only fair to allow such marriages to be considered voidable (open to challenge by the other spouse) in a situation where a person discovered, after the ceremony, that their spouse was of the same biological sex. This right of challenge should be based on the notion of deception and not simply on the grounds of the inability to consummate the marriage. Of course, if that is to be the case, it leads to the conclusion that whatever the new birth certificate may say, we are prepared to look behind it. Personal identity cannot completely be altered.[14]

---

13. *B v France* above, note 10 above.
14. Rodney Holder, an Anglican curate who cautiously advocates transsexual marriage and child adoption, nevertheless accepts that with regard to birth certificates, 'some form of protection ought to be afforded a spouse against deception'. See *Crucible*, July–September (1998), p.132.

3. Care of Children

There are two sets of circumstances in which transsexuals may be involved in the care of children. Some will have become biological parents as the result of a relationship in their original gender role. Others will wish to become parents in their new gender role by adopting a child. In the case of a female-to-male transsexual, the female partner could try donor insemination.

The practice of donor insemination is regulated by the *Human Fertilisation and Embryology Act 1990*. Under that Act, if an unmarried couple go together for treatment, the male partner will in law be treated as the father of any child conceived by donor insemination. This again raises the issue of personal identity. A recent European decision[15] has again used biological criteria to establish who is eligible to be treated as a father, thereby excluding the female-to-male transsexual. However, such a person might well be granted a residence order if this were deemed appropriate and necessary.

In law, adoption is available either to married couples jointly or to single persons.[16] A cohabiting couple may not apply together (although one may apply alone to adopt and the other seek a residence order). Presumably, this could also happen in the case where one partner was a transsexual. A recent leading decision has held that there is no reason in law why a homosexual person should not be allowed to adopt a child;[17] the same reasoning would probably apply to a transsexual. However, adoption practice and the backgrounds of the children available for adoption may be far more significant than the law in this area. There are virtually no small healthy babies available for adoption in the UK at the present time and most adoptions are of older, difficult or handicapped children. Though some people argue that the idea of a 'non-standard' family caring for such a child may actually

---

15. *X, Y and Z* v *UK* [1997] 2 Fam Law Rep 892.
16. *Adoption Act 1976*.
17. *Re W (homosexual adopter)* [1997] 2 Fam Law Rep 406.

be much better than no family at all, there is something morally objectionable about the suggestion that these children might not suffer in the same way as a healthy baby might. The real issue, which remains to be addressed, is whether the emotional dysfunction of a family can damage the emotional development of children.

Contact with Existing Children

The decision by a married person to effect a change of gender usually precipitates the end of the marriage. If there are children, the usual decisions must be made about where they will live and how much contact they will have with the other parent. There is nothing in law preventing a transsexual person from being the primary carer after a divorce. For example, in one case[18] the mother suffered a serious breakdown after hearing that her husband was contemplating a gender change. Following a period in care, the children went to live with their father. The court, ruling on another aspect of this case, held that, although the situation was 'bizarre', it did not appear to be against the girls' best interests to be cared for by this parent. This, however, is not the usual picture. More often than not transsexual parents lose contact with their offspring altogether. Some judges simply report that transsexual parents accepted that they would never be allowed face-to-face contact with their children.[19] One Court of Appeal decision described the situation as 'tragic' but declined to force contact on an unwilling child who claimed he no longer had a father.[20] In yet another case, the court said it would not insist on contact if this would be too distressing for the mother.[21]

These decisions go against the prevailing view that contact is almost always in the best interests of children if there is no threat

---

18. *Re H-S (minors)* [1994] 3 All ER 390.
19. For example, *Re L (Contact: Transsexual applicant)* [1995] 2 Fam Law Rep 438.
20. *Re F (Minors) (Denial of Contact)* [1993] 2 Fam Law Rep 677.
21. *Re J (Minors)* 2nd October 1997 (unreported).

of significant harm to them. The courts have probably been rather quick to jump to conclusions about the difficulties of a continuing relationship between transsexual parents and their offspring. In practice, the loss altogether of a loving parent may be more detrimental than contact with a parent who has changed gender. However, it is very difficult to draw up any general recommendations governing this area of family law where so much depends on the particular facts of individual cases and the court's perception of the notoriously elusive concept of the 'best interests of the child'.

4. *Prisons*

The small but significant number of transsexuals who commit crimes raises particular questions of personal identity in that a decision must be made where to incarcerate them (and in some cases whether to continue to supply the hormones they have been receiving). A pragmatic approach is generally preferred and the Association of Chief Police Officers is presently working on detailed guidelines to cover this situation.[22]

Discrimination

This is an area of the law that has received considerable attention recently and it is therefore unlikely that the government's review will recommend any significant amendments. Following a decision of the European Court of Human Rights,[23] it was held that the *Equal Treatment Directive* applied to transsexuals who are the subject of discrimination at work on the grounds of their change of sex (NB change of *sex* assumed). Subsequent English cases have followed this approach and the *Sex Discrimination (Gender Reassignment) Regulations 1999* have now amended the

---

22. *Hansard* written answers: 9th December 1997; 6th May 1999.
23. *P v S and Cornwall* [1996] All ER (EC) 397.

Sex Discrimination Act 1975 and prohibited discrimination on the grounds of transsexuality in employment or vocational training.[24]

The possibility may arise in the future where, for example, a pastoral care worker in a church setting decides to change gender. In such a situation a crisis would presumably be precipitated and the church might well wish to dismiss the transsexual employee. As the law stands, the issue is far from clear. *The Sex Discrimination Act 1975* provides a specific exception for priests: 'where the employment is limited to one sex so as to comply with the doctrines of the religion, or avoid offending the religious susceptibilities of a significant number of its followers'.[25] That does not, however, cover a church worker. The grounds for dismissal would not, of course, be that the person was now male instead of female (or vice versa), but rather the breach of church standards which might prohibit any attempt to 'change sex', i.e. discrimination on grounds of moral standards rather than 'sex' per se. Whether the church could argue that case successfully in the face of legislation that specifically prohibits discrimination on grounds of transsexuality remains an open question. It should be mentioned that the new *Human Rights Act 1998* does require courts to have special regard to the collective rights of religious organisations.[26] Therefore, an argument could conceivably be mounted that if the organisation found it contrary to its moral beliefs to employ a transsexual person, this might just fall within the exemption dealing with priests.

A further question may well be raised as to whether evidence will be required by a church to the effect that persons seeking to be married are of the same biological sex as their presenting gender, and if so what it would be. This may come to be a very

---

24. In a recent case a male-to-female transsexual, previously sacked as a nonconformist church minister, faced practical problems in her new role as a trainee beautician since models refused to work with her. She is now being allowed to pursue a claim for compensation for loss of earnings on the grounds of sexual discrimination, as reported in *The Times*, 16th March 2000.
25. s. 19.
26. s. 13.

real issue, for since passports can now be amended to indicate an assumed gender identity, passports as such would hardly measure up to the kind of reliable evidence concerned churches would presumably require. Were birth certificates similarly to be amended the problems posed may seem to become virtually insurmountable. In this connection a potential, nevertheless very real, dilemma may increasingly be posed for church authorities.[27]

---

27. A recent case reported in the *Daily Mail*, 29th February 2000, involved a married female teacher at a Roman Catholic secondary school who wished to continue in her role except presenting as a man, following gender reassignment treatment. After taking legal advice, the school governors decided that they had no alternative but to recognise the teacher's right to change her gender, though the decision has apparently caused concerned reactions from parents. The *Daily Mail* of 4th May 2000 reported a case where the owner of a public house was required to pay compensation to a transsexual whom he held responsible for the decline of regular customers. The case highlighted the implication for all businesses that provide goods and services to ensure they develop equal opportunities policies that cover transsexuals, or face the prospect of possible discrimination claims backed by the Equal Opportunities Commission.

5

The Perspective of Scripture

It is undeniable that a small but significant number of people maintain that there is a contradiction between the gender they *feel* that they are and the gender their apparent biology *says* that they are. Why should society not accede to their demands to be treated in accordance with what they feel themselves to be? Why should they not, where necessary, undergo surgery and other medical treatment to 'bring their bodies into line'? From a biblical perspective then, how should we view the issues of gender reassignment in general and gender reassignment surgery in particular? Should post-operative transsexuals be able to change their birth certificate and be allowed to marry?

Evangelical Christianity rests on the conviction that God has revealed his intentions for human life in the Bible. This is why, in seeking answers to questions relating to ethics, we begin with the 'Maker's instructions'. In what ways does God guide human understanding through Scripture? Does the Bible have anything to say to us concerning these issues?

The many different and sometimes contradictory responses to this question show that this is not always an entirely straightforward exercise. We need to beware of attempts to indulge in simplistic moral readings of the Bible that treat it as a sort of ethical cookbook. For example, Deuteronomy 23:1 clearly states: 'No-one who has been emasculated by crushing or cutting may enter the assembly of the LORD.' Some have immediately drawn the conclusion that the Bible therefore outlaws practices such as gender reassignment surgery, and that no more need be said on the subject. Others have highlighted Deuteronomy 22:5 which appears to prohibit cross-dressing, or 1 Corinthians 6:9–11 where Paul (according to the King James Version) appears to condemn those who behave in an effeminate manner.

To leap to such conclusions, however, can result in misuse of the Bible and a failure to do justice to the complexities of responsible exegesis and application. For a start, in relation to Deuteronomy 23:1, there is a clear progression in Scripture which culminates in the implied acceptance of the genitally-mutilated by Jesus in Matthew 19:12, and the conversion, baptism and acceptance into the kingdom of God of the Ethiopian eunuch in Acts 8:26-39.[1] On this basis, some have suggested that, far from outlawing gender reassignment surgery, the witness of the New Testament actually supports it. But, as the context shows, the NIV is right to translate Matthew 19:12 as 'those who have renounced marriage' (literally 'those who have made themselves eunuchs' (cf. KJV). As the context shows, Jesus' comments are made in direct response to a question about marriage. He is not commending self-castration.[2] Similarly, 1 Corinthians 6:9 is now recognised as referring to young male prostitutes[3] and therefore has little relevance to our present discussion.

Whilst some Christians see Deuteronomy 22:5 as a clear reference to divine condemnation of transsexuality, most commentators suggest that this passage contains minimal relevance to the debate at all, or indeed to twentieth-century society. It is

---

1. Also most commentators accept that Isaiah 56:4–5 removes the ban on the genetically mutilated being admitted to 'the assembly of the Lord'. See, for example, P.D. Hanson, *Isaiah 40–66* (Louisville: John Knox Press, 1995), p.194.
2. See W.D. Davies and D.C. Allison, *The Gospel According to Saint Matthew* (vol. III of The International Critical Commentary Series, Edinburgh: T&T Clark, 1997), pp.23–4; also D.A. Hagner, *Matthew 14–28* (Dallas: Word, 1995), p.550.
3. See G.D. Fee, *The First Epistle to the Corinthians* (Grand Rapids: Eerdmans, 1987), p.243.

likely that, in keeping with God's covenantal concern to preserve the holiness of his character reflected within the covenant community of Israel, and to avoid anything which threatened Israel's existence and harmony, the cross-dressing prohibition was introduced to prevent involvement on the part of Israelites in contemporary Canaanite religious rituals of the day, which involved swapping of sex roles and cross-dressing.[4] Whatever the significance of this particular verse, it is probably doing a disservice to reasonable hermeneutics to apply it directly to transsexuals. Nevertheless, the strength of the Hebrew word translated as 'abomination' or 'detests' indicates that in the sight of God such practices were fundamentally incompatible with the identity of God's people, and therefore it remains likely that Deuteronomy 22:5 is intended to signify a reaffirmation of divine intent, in that the sanctity of the distinctiveness between the two created sexes is to be maintained.[5]

Individual passages, such as Deuteronomy 23:1, do have something relevant to say to us therefore. The regulation in this verse supports and affirms the positive value of sex and explicitly contradicts the dualistic suggestion that sexuality and spirituality are somehow in opposition to one another. But it is wrong to isolate that verse from the rest of Scripture. We must remember to view the teaching of Scripture as a whole as we seek to discover

---

4. See W.A. VanGemeren (gen. ed.), *The New International Dictionary of Old Testament Theology and Exegesis* IV (5 vols; Carlisle: Paternoster Press, 1996), pp.314–18.

5. Ibid., p.316. We accept that to some extent the question is begged here: was cross-dressing prohibited because it was Canaanite, or was the Canaanite ritual prohibited because it involved cross-dressing? Similarly, did Jeremiah deplore child-sacrifice merely because it was Baalite, or because it encouraged, inter alia, child-sacrifice? Yahweh was presumably unlikely to have been comfortable with his people cross-dressing if only it could have been freed from unfortunate religious associations, and we need to be careful not to dilute Scripture at this point. The connection between cross-dressing and religion is, of course, very significant. There is a profound psychological connection between forms of sexual anomism and certain religious roles. Here we wish to highlight, not relativise the fundamental ethical significance.

principles and approaches to guide our thinking and decision-making. The themes of creation, fall, redemption and final restoration provide one helpful framework in this respect.

The theme of *creation* emphasises the truth that this is God's world and that in bringing it into being God declared it to be 'good'.[6] The presence of so much that runs contrary to the will of God is explained by the theme of the *fall*. God's initiative to put things right again is the theme of *redemption*, which finds its chief focus in the life, death and resurrection of Jesus Christ. The theme of *final restoration* helps us to understand that although the transformation of creation has begun, full restoration will not take place until final judgment and the end of time, as we now know it.

How do these themes help us in thinking about transsexuality?

The Doctrine of Creation

The doctrine of *creation* with the story of Adam and Eve, and the insistence that 'male and female he created them',[7] shows that our sexual identity is part of the 'givenness' of how we have been made. It is not therefore something that we can select for ourselves on the basis simply of how we feel. A Christian understanding of morality firmly resists the idea that human beings are somehow completely in charge of their own destiny and can justifiably exclude the Creator and his purposes from their experiences of life.

Genesis 1:27 also emphasises the basic and clear distinction between men and women. It does not teach, as some allege, that maleness and femaleness are two poles between which is a spectrum or ambiguous blend of human sexuality. This at least suggests that the individual who claims ontologically to be 'a woman trapped in a man's body' (or vice versa) is fundamentally

---

6. For example, Genesis 1:4.
7. Genesis 1:27.

mistaken given the biblical assertion of the priority of the physical. Whether such an individual should nevertheless have the freedom to undergo gender reassignment surgery on other grounds is, of course, a different question. The point is that a Christian understanding of what it is to be human cannot easily take at face value an individual's claim that their 'true sex' may be different from their birth sex as indicated by their chromosomes, gonads and external genitalia. Sex is so fundamental to human existence that it cannot be dissected out and viewed in isolation. Whilst it is true that the appearance of sexually-differentiated gonads and external genitalia is part of a process of development, this is not the case at the sex chromosomal level since these are, in the vast majority of cases, clearly either XX or XY from the outset.

The early chapters of Genesis also set out the foundation of the Christian understanding of marriage as one of God's gracious gifts to humanity. Relationships that are heterosexual, monogamous and open to the possibility of procreation are clearly God's revealed ideal for the expression of sexuality, a point particularly emphasised in Genesis 2:18–25. This is the basis for the Christian understanding of what marriage is all about. Some have argued that relationships in which one or both partners is a post-operative transsexual and which enshrine most of what marriage offers should also be regarded as 'marriage'. This argument is all the stronger since procreation, for example, is not generally seen as essential to marriage. Infertility as such is no bar to matrimony. It can therefore be argued that a childless relationship need not preclude the partners concerned from being regarded as a married couple.

However apparently loving and mutually supportive a transsexual relationship may be, and however much society may be justified in wishing to offer such relationships the same freedoms and privileges that married couples enjoy, efforts to elevate them to the status of biblical marriage itself should be resisted on the grounds stated earlier. Such a relationship cannot be regarded as truly being contracted between a man and a woman as it is really between two partners of the same sex, one of whom has opted to adopt a gender identity that is at variance with their biological sex. Such a relationship might justifiably be viewed, if not as tantamount to a homosexual partnership, then at least as a deceptive representation of an apparent heterosexual relationship. This is arguably more subtle and devious than an overt homosexual relationship. When a male-to-female transsexual chooses to present as a lesbian woman and quite legally seeks to marry someone of the opposite birth sex,[8] issues of falsehood, manipulation and deviousness become blatant and potentially offensive. Similar principles apply where two transsexuals of opposite biological sex wish to marry and live as a bona fide heterosexual couple. Likewise, although divorce in a partnership involving a pre-operative transsexual may be seen as justifiable on other grounds, we should resist the suggestion that such a marriage should be annulled on the basis that the partners are really the same sex. However individuals choose to behave, their sex cannot be satisfactorily demonstrated to be other than that which their biology dictates. Indeed, some transsexual people do accept that, for example in the case of a male-to-female transsexual, a man chooses to *present* himself as a woman and does not become a woman with gender reassignment surgery.

The Doctrine of the Fall

The doctrine of the *fall* leads us to expect that distortions in God's pattern for living will be present in the world as a direct result of human choices to ignore God's instructions and also indirectly through the effects of sin on creation as a whole. Adam and Eve's disobedience had a profound effect on the rest of creation.

A further strand in Scripture is represented by God's provision of law, given partly as a means of limiting the consequences of human sin. Nothing is said directly about the issue of transsexuality, although notwithstanding the likely contextual factors,

---

8. See p.37.

behaviour that confuses the distinctions between the sexes is clearly forbidden.

Recognising and acknowledging aspects of our fallen condition does not mean legitimising them, as some have tried to argue. Rather it involves seeking to bring our tarnished lives into line with what we believe to be the revealed will and purposes of God.

The Doctrine of Redemption

The doctrine of *redemption* encourages us to realise that putting things right is central to how God is involved in his creation now. This is how those who suffer may find hope, a hope based on the healing work of Jesus Christ and his offer of 'life in all its fullness'[9] for all who turn to him in repentance and faith. Fundamental to the idea of repentance is a switch from the self-centredness that mars and distorts so much of our human experience, not least in the area of our sexuality, to a life which seeks to be governed primarily by God's purposes and standards.

The Doctrine of Final Restoration

The doctrine of *final restoration* warns us, however, that although the complete overthrow of sin and all its effects is most certainly on God's agenda, our present experience of his healing work is often necessarily partial and incomplete. The fulfilment of our redemption awaits a future existence beyond the present world.

As has already been noted, controversial debate surrounds the question of the causation of transsexuality.[10] Many resist the demands of transsexuals with the claim that the 'condition' is

---

9. See John 10:10.
10. See p.15.

purely psychological in origin, and that their perceived gender confusion has no basis in reality. If the implication is that others are expected to collude in the projection of an illusion, then whatever transsexuals may feel and say, their real gender is what their body evidences. The case for accepting gender reassignment is correspondingly weakened, as is the case for making changes to an individual's birth certificate. It might be felt appropriate to allow other identity documents to reflect the gender individuals perceive themselves to be now, but the gender recorded at the time of birth is a matter of historical fact that should not therefore be amended.

On the other hand, if the cause could be shown to be physiological (or as some transsexuals prefer to suggest, 'medical') then we might be able to conclude that a transsexual has the brain or psychology of one sex and the body of the other. In this situation, the claim that 'I am a woman trapped in a male body' (or vice versa) might be true and there might therefore be a case for concluding that an individual's apparent gender is not the whole story. It has been pointed out previously that the present state of research indicates that the precise aetiology of transsexuality is still an open question. Nevertheless, the onus of proof is on those who wish to change the status quo, and despite some claims to the contrary, it remains to be demonstrated that transsexuality has a physiological cause.

Probably the chief argument employed nowadays in favour of gender reassignment surgery is that it would enable what is popularly perceived to be the basic human right of self-determination to be expressed more fully. Our society values individual freedom of choice very highly and frowns on the injustice of situations where such freedom is limited.[11] However, there are plenty of circumstances in which society chooses to restrict a

---

11. This raises a major ethical issue concerning the assumed human right of absolute self-determination. We do not attempt to become involved in this study in the wide-ranging philosophical discussion regarding the validity of extreme individualist claims, however it will be evident that this report effectively rejects such claims on biblical grounds.

person's liberty, either out of concern for the individual's welfare or in order to protect others in society.[12] If it were true that the aetiology of transsexuality has a significant psychological component, then our responsibility to those who were to be seen as suffering from this disorder would include the need at the very least to exercise caution before allowing them unfettered exercise of such freedom. As an incidental point, if a biological aetiology could be proved (which we believe is unlikely), a question would inevitably arise with regard to the preferred option of 'corrective' treatment.

We also need to bear in mind the dangers of manipulation by unscrupulous clinicians preying on a particularly vulnerable section of the population. Gender reassignment surgery is far from being the magic 'cure-all' it is sometimes presented to be. The post-operative transsexual lifestyle requires the regular assistance of hormone therapy throughout its lifetime to sustain it successfully. Post-operative transsexuals report high levels of stress and depression, and, although definitive statistics are not available, it is thought a small but nevertheless significant and disturbing minority seek to return to their original gender role. In such cases gender reassignment surgery has manifestly failed to deliver its promised benefits and, far from bringing the body and psyche into unity, has actually led to more pain and confusion as deep-rooted causal factors that have not been addressed remain.

It must be emphasised that successful adjustment to non-surgical solutions has been reported in a significant number of cases. For Christians the holistic psychosomatic unity offered as an intrinsic aspect of the healing gospel of Jesus Christ represents unquestionably the preferred route to peace of mind and body.

It is clear from the perspective of many transsexuals that, with notable exceptions, the church has appeared strong on condemnation and weak on compassion when dealing with those who

---

12. For example, with the age of consent; car driving limitations; people with mental health problems, etc.

wrestle with these issues.[13] In standing against the prevailing 'me-first' culture of our society and the virtual deification of sex, the church should have much to offer. An observation by Dame Cicely Saunders about euthanasia is relevant here:

> If you relieve a person's pain and if you can make him feel like a wanted person, then you are not going to be asked about euthanasia . . . I think euthanasia is an admission of defeat, and a totally negative approach. One should be working to see that it is not needed.[14]

The challenge for the church is to help society substitute 'gender reassignment surgery' for 'euthanasia' in this challenging statement.

---

13. Although it is worth pointing out that emotive cliché and hostile caricature frequently distort the true picture. It is perhaps a sobering thought that it has proved virtually impossible, for example, to identify a single church that has gone on record with any 'strong condemnation' of transsexual surgery.

14. Quoted by P. Ramsey, *Ethics at the Edge of Life* (Yale University Press, 1978), p.152.

6

An Ethical Perspective on Transsexuality

In this section we consider some of the major issues raised by the present debate on transsexuality from a Christian ethical perspective.

The Importance of Understanding Sex and Gender, Male and Female

Right at the outset we think it is vitally important that we retain a conceptual distinction between *sex* and *gender*. This has been a universally accepted distinction in the past, but self-conscious ideological movements and a lack of conceptual clarity are eroding it. For example, those who design public survey forms that invite us to give our 'gender' and not our 'sex' help confuse the issue. We consider that in the face of misapprehension caused by a tendency to conflate sex and gender, there is a strong theological motivation for desiring to maintain the distinction.[1]

---

1. It is appreciated that in the contemporary world sex-gender separation has become a controversial topic; but of course it is equally controversial not to separate sex and gender. It is 'fashionable' nowadays in a world where individual rights are deemed to be inviolable to regard *sex* as a 'construct'. But at that point the debate about transgender issues ceases to be *ethical* and becomes purely *political*,

Christians do not simply wish to legitimate perceived gender-role distinctions or differentiations because they point to a binary distinction amongst human beings – some evidently have no moral significance, and some are actually oppressive and worthy of censure. Yet we *do* claim that the binary distinctions, however distorted, point towards a significant and fundamental truth: humanity is made male and female, and that male and female are complementary within the common experience of human existence. Indeed, gender roles are often distorted precisely at the point where this complementary aspect is most obviously disrupted. This belief derives from a theology of creation, and despite contemporary pressures, Christians point to the continuing experience of Jewish, Christian, and other communities as a basis for the practical outworking of the experience of this binary distinction in human nature as both good and fulfilling. Of course, some aspects of that message may seem unintelligible to the world outside the Church, but at least Christians are starting from the right kind of foundation. We then need to be clear that if the Christian doctrine of creation, and specifically of the creation of humanity, is correct, it might be expected that some practical indications of it might be seen in the ordinary experience of people, and even in psychobiological investigations, as we would expect to interpret scientific research within patterns of thought grounded in Christian Scripture and tradition.

The implication is that Christians should be living, and encouraging others to live, in ways that respect the loving creative

---

(*cont.*) which, as we have seen, is precisely what the postmodern agenda of those who promote 'sex as a construct' constitutes. Frequently in contemporary public debates concerning issues like transsexuality or homosexuality we are urged to lay aside moral considerations to concentrate purely on the legal and political dimensions. Those who press for primacy of the moral dimension are typically and pejoratively labelled as 'the moralists' who just make people feel guilty and consequently deserve to be ignored! In this report we do not accept the modern preoccupation with separating moral and legal aspects, and unashamedly hold out for this being a fundamentally ethical issue where responsibilities rather than rights assume greatest importance, with the Judeo-Christian doctrine of creation remaining supremely relevant.

will of the creator God for the creation. This encouragement of others is an encouragement grounded in outgoing Christian love, and showing that by living in such ways people may draw closer to the good that God intends for them. The motivation for the Christian message is precisely for the sake of the people to whom the gospel is addressed – Christians are not interested in abstract principles, nor are they engaged in a political power-game to get others to live in accordance with their rules. The distinction of sex and gender allows the acknowledgement of the relativity of gender experience and the social problems of gender, whilst maintaining that being human involves being male or female, and does not ignore the fact that some controversial implications remain from the contemporary application of biblical teachings.

We are convinced of the validity of the basic assertion that 'male and female' is a distinction of *sex*, and that the conceptual appropriation of that distinction into perceptions of nature and roles provides the related distinction of *gender*. It is not possible to do without either, but for the benefit of humanity it is essential to keep them apart because:

1. Conflating them to the level of *sex* threatens to confirm and objectify oppressive or entirely contingent distinctions.
2. Conflating them to the level of *gender* threatens to relativise to the point where an objectively significant aspect of human life is believed to be almost infinitely plastic.

How Should We Regard Transsexuality?

The word 'transsexual' can be misleading. It implies that there is some form of personal alienation at the level of *sex*, but is not specific concerning the nature or content of that alienation. There is a sense in which the phrase 'a woman in a man's body' (or 'a man in a woman's body') sums up the popular perception quite well, but does so only by begging the questions that actually require answers before a proper analysis can begin.

We need to start by distinguishing between sex-*ambiguity* as a physiological fact at birth (the phenomenon of the 'intersex' or 'hermaphrodite' state constituting examples of such ambiguity), and transsexual phenomena. Something which is ambiguous between two distinct things, and where ambiguity is regarded as bad, will need to be resolved if possible into one or other of these distinct possibilities; this process of resolution usually takes place in the rare individual cases of sex-ambiguity without 'transsexual' issues ever arising. The 'error' of sex-identification in the famous *Joel/Joella* case,[2] has given rise to a recasting of the subsequent discussion in the light of its implications.

In this regard, it is essential to reflect systematically concerning the kind of claim that belief in 'transsex' constitutes.

1. There are a variety of indicators used to determine the sex of human beings. These are familiar and well documented.
2. There are a variety of social and cultural expectations and beliefs that are used to organise self-perceptions as regards sex-identity. Some of these are self-consciously mere discriminators, setting up arbitrary social distinctions between 'male' and 'female', whilst others are believed to follow in non-arbitrary ways from sex difference. This is the arena of conscious reception and interpretation of sex, which is to say that it operates at the level of *gender*.

We should note that the common 'transsexual claim' that a person can be 'a woman in a man's body' (or 'a man in a woman's body') is firstly a claim about supposed *reality*. It is not a claim about the freedom of a person to do what he or she likes with the body, nor is it a claim that 'male' and 'female' are entirely arbitrary labels corresponding to no element of reality. Nevertheless, such claims may well be held and believed in by some

---

2. Where a girl was misidentified and registered at birth as a boy, but was allowed to change her birth certificate ten years later. Described by experts as a 'medical mistake'. See, for example, *The Guardian*, Wednesday, 2nd December 1998.

people, and they may become associated with moves towards recognising the phenomenon of the transsexual, because this recognition will give greater political space for acceptance of the kind of plasticity of human identity which the 'non-realist' desires.

Assessing the Transsexual Claim

We would like to look more closely at the reality of the transsexual claim. Some people have taken the claim seriously and have searched for a basis for the truth for it in the individual, perhaps in neurophysiology. A proper reading of this approach is simply to see it as extending the range of sex criteria (e.g. internal and external genitalia, chromosomes, etc.) by adding further indicative criteria to them. In this sense, the basis of sex identification is allowed to become more complex, but no different in principle from sex identification, as currently understood.

What is intriguing in the context of the present study is the way in which discoveries in (say) neurophysiology are being allowed by some authors to 'trump' any other evidence, and to be admitted as more valid pointers towards 'true' sex. Why should this be so? It *is* so, we suggest, because the authors concerned have already made a *prima facie* commitment, perhaps for genuinely compassionate reasons, to the subjective reports of the persons concerned. It is because of these reports that the authors seek for a basis in reality of the reported experience. However, some difficulties emerge.

In the first place, which takes precedence, the physiological evidence or the subjective report? If the truth of maleness or femaleness is held to be independent of the experience of it (which is, of course, necessary if it is possible to be *wrong* about one's sex) then physiology *must* come first. If the subjective report comes first, then no amount of evidence, ostensibly to back up the report can do more than precisely *back it up* – the report comes first. What it *is* to be male or female becomes a matter of what it is to *feel* male or female!

The second difficulty is that by presenting the matter in the terms outlined, the authors who seek for a 'cause' of transsexual experience effectively commit themselves beforehand to there being some determinate essential 'thing' deserving of the unitary label 'transsexuality'. The point here is crucial and often misunderstood. It has a parallel with the issues of *essentialism* and social *constructivism* in debates about homosexuality. 'Homosexual' is often assumed to be a psychobiological label for a 'caused condition'. 'Transsexual' is being threatened with the same fate. An important question that needs to be raised is whether, contrary to common assumptions, there is any such essential 'medical thing' as 'transsexualism' at all? The majority of pathologists do not raise this question. They tend to assume that the essentialist position is true and then discover a basis for it.[3]

For the sake of clarity, we describe three ways in which the transsexual case is commonly expressed, and examine the implications to highlight what are the real underlying issues.

In the first instance, the transsexual typically may feel that they are 'a woman in a man's body' or vice versa. Medico-biological investigation reveals evidence that the range of indicators for sex typology (extended to include factors such as neurophysiological development) have some 'male' and some 'female' associated elements. The *truth* of the claim must now be assessed. On traditional assessment, the sex is unambiguous; genitalia are perfectly formed, the person is fertile. However, it is considered that perhaps 'new evidence' should now be allowed to 'trump' these traditional verdicts. Such a practical outcome almost inevitably surrenders to a form of *gnosticism*[4] in which individuals are effectively offered the right to determine their own sex in disregard of the discovered evidence. A failure to recognise this has caused some commentators to become completely confused and admit total plasticity with regard to *sex* and *gender*.

---

3. The position adopted in this report prefers to adopt the view that 'transsexuality' as such is a form of social construct than an actual medical 'condition'.
4. For a definition see the section on terminology p.2.

A second way transsexuals often express themselves is by claiming to be a female 'soul' or 'spirit' attached to a male body, or vice versa. Christians find this dualistic claim that separates soul and body a problem, particularly as it appears to adopt Gnostic concepts to legitimate in theological terms the notion of 'a woman in a man's body'. Orthodox Christian thinking resists the removal of 'true sex' from the physical realm and the implicit resentment or rejection of physical creation.[5]

A third expression of the transsexual claim may be found in the form of gender-sex confusion. 'Confusion' in this case does not mean 'error' or 'mistake' in any simple sense. Effectively the individual feels 'alienated' in some important way from the truth of his or her being. It may be possible to point to a causal account for this alienation. One such account might point towards pathologies in the social construction of gender roles in a culture. In other words, individuals have become alienated from assigned gender roles determined by birth-sex through entirely gratuitous or actual false associations of sex and gender. For example, a girl likes some 'boys'' sport which girls are not allowed to play. She does not like 'girls'' sports. She discovers a liking for mathematics and physics, which are 'male' things. The boys, unable to react to her as a girl because she fails to conform to their stereotypes, and because they have insufficient imagination to escape them, treat her as an 'honorary boy'. Such a relatively trivial account, where the factors may be sufficiently obvious and public to imply little basis of long-term harm, may now be taken over and adopted as a basis for reflection on more insidious forms of gender-sex confusion.

We do not suggest that *all* of the phenomena relating to transsexuality belong to such a category as the third example.

---

5. Amongst the oddities of this conception may be mentioned the gender-polarisation of souls. Traditionally souls have been considered sexless (or conventionally feminine, as in the Greek ψυχή or Latin *anima*), though in some later speculation (e.g. Augustine), they were bi-sexual, *animus* and *anima*. However, the notion that a man (normally) has a male soul and a woman a female soul is very odd.

But it would be inconceivable to imagine that none of them did. The first and second examples have similar elements as they depend upon some 'medical' basis being found for the experience of alienation from assigned sex. However, we believe that the dangers of using account one as a basis for assigning 'true' sex are far-reaching because it constitutes a different order of claim entirely.

Ethical Implications Raised by Transsexuality

Experience of sex/gender alienation of the self[6] is undoubtedly a complex phenomenon, and 'real', at least in the sense that many people *experience* some measure of such alienation. The Christian gospel is one of reconciliation and peace. It points towards the truth that human beings really *are* alienated! One form of that alienation is undoubtedly alienation from self, and one aspect of *that* alienation is sex/gender alienation.[7]

We may affirm two things at this point:

1. Our *culture* bears a responsibility for its adoption of false gender roles and distinctions, and for its false evaluation of those distinctions. This is emphatically *not* a simple repudiation of inequalities of opportunity in education or employment! Christians will necessarily view the significance of this responsibility as *theological*. The reality and purpose of sex difference is grounded in creation, and the gendered perception of sexual meaning ought to co-ordinate with God's purposes.
2. All people (including Christians) are called to redemption and sanctification in their being as sexed creatures, as male

---

6. Arguably a better, though more cumbersome, description of 'transsexuality'.
7. The degree of seriousness with which this 'alienation' is regarded depends on one's theology of sexual distinction and difference, and the ultimacy of sexual differentiation.

and female. Persistently tempted to borrow their understandings of the significance and meaning of sexual being as male or female from sources which are themselves radically alienated from God who is Lord of all creation, it would therefore be unsurprising if these 'understandings' were not themselves forms of self-alienation.

As we therefore do not believe it is possible to avoid a commitment both to the truth of sexual distinction and to the relation of that distinction to human existence as a psychophysiological reality, we may therefore affirm further:

3. *Sex* is fundamental to being human; each person is, inevitably, male or female. Sometimes the process of sexual typology is not straightforward, as the 'intersex' case has shown.[8] But that merely confirms sexual typology to be a matter of interpretation of a reality distinct from the judgement made.
4. *Gender* is the social appropriation of sex and its meaning at the level of conceptualisation, i.e. in the life of the mind. No self-understanding of sexual identity as male or female, and no experience of sexual self-alienation, can be thought or expressed without the language and categories supplied by gender distinction.
5. Our 'identity' is certainly not a matter entirely of our own making. How *much* we may legitimately 'make ourselves' is controversial in Christian theology. Our *sex*, at least, is a part of our identity given to and not made by us. Because it is fundamental, it is not an historical phenomenon. It is not subject to development. We do not actually *become* male or female. Our male/femaleness 'unfolds' in a progression from genotype to phenotype. Although this is acknowledged to be a controversial assertion, and some experts who are committed to the development of the

---

8. See p.22.

concept may well resent rejection of the 'becoming' of sexual identity, we nevertheless make our assertion at least in part on the basis of Psalm 139.[9]

6. We have at least acknowledged the hypothetical possibility that a coherent account of alienation at the fundamental level of assigned sex might at some time in the future be sustainable. If what it *is* to be sexed as male or female is a fact of biology,[10] it is *possible* to conceive that the received interpretation of the biological data may be wrong, or that all of the biological facts may not be being assessed. But we should note that it is from such a hypothetical possibility that reassessment of the usual criteria for typing sex and the established confidence in using those criteria is being demanded.

7. We believe, nevertheless, that the outcome of the reassessment and reflection being demanded should not be allowed to privilege the self-consciousness of the individual because:

(a) sex is then made subjective, contingent and historicised,
(b) there is an implicit endorsement of a new form of *gnosticism*.

Hence, even though it is hypothetically possible that the criteria for sexual typology may develop, and the catalyst for that development may be individual experiences of alienation from their apparent sex, it is axiomatic that the reality of our sexuality is not immediately given in our feelings. The reality of ourselves, including the reality of our own sex, is a matter of *public* observation. In this, as in every matter to do with ourselves, we have to learn from others how to know ourselves. Privileged private perceptions have to be aligned with public perceptions. Although like any scientific process, biological investigation

---

9. Especially vv. 13–16.
10. Since what it is to be *human* involves physical being, there seems no reason to resist this claim.

can go astray, nevertheless here it acts as a guardian for the principle of public objectivity.

8. Much experience of sex-alienation seems rooted in gender-perception. Whilst alienation is undoubtedly bad, we believe the grounds of reconciliation ought to be the truth, i.e. the truth of a person's *sex*, and not false *gender*-beliefs. The process of reconciliation we are referring to here may involve changes in patterns of thought and behaviour, and may also involve much wider re-thinking of gender distinction on the part of the relevant culture and society.

9. For some people, the question of alienation will be acknowledged as a problem of receiving and acknowledging the truth; their 'problem' will be understood as one of false consciousness, not of anything false about the body. Accordingly, someone may, for example, resort to prayer in order to seek to understand more fully what it is to be male, given his feelings of 'being female'. Such people will have accepted the truth of the claim that sex is 'given', and also the specific truth that their particular sex is whatever-it-is; their feelings of alienation from that are a challenging issue to be worked through. For some others, on the other hand, the alienation of feelings and sex will resolve themselves into what can only really be characterised as an aggressive intent against the body, a kind of 'body-resentment' that relies upon privileging feelings over physical reality, and resolves into a determination or obsession to physically correlate the body with the feelings of sex-identity generated through various gendered self-understandings. The incipient *gnosticism* of this view has already been highlighted. It shows up not merely in its claim to a basis of knowledge that cannot be tested and checked by any public criteria, but also in its treatment of the physical as a manipulable tool to the realisation of the purposes of the supposedly 'true self'.

10. For Christians, the response to alienation represented by such *gnostic* tendencies is fundamentally unacceptable

because it represents a subjective denial of the true basis of the self in the objective good reality of God's creation. The fundamentals of human identity are given and not chosen, even if 'choice' acquires the character of a kind of 'self-intuited necessity', as in the case of a person whose psyche is so transfixed on the feeling of 'being female' (although in a man's body) that the idea achieves a kind of unshakeable subjective grasp. The ideal Christian response involves commending and supporting the humble process of self-discovery outlined above.

The Question of Intersex

Some comment is appropriate regarding whether the paradigm of physical *intersex* is speculatively extensible to include the typical transsexual.

A definitive medical 'intersex' condition, such as occurred in the *Joel/Joella* case[11] cannot in our view be considered as in any way comparable to the transsexual claim of wanting to be recognised as really 'a man in a woman's body' or vice versa. In this study a clear distinction has been maintained between 'transsexuality' and 'intersex', but much current thinking appears to emphasise and even accept a hypothetical situation of people surviving to adulthood in a kind of 'intersex' state, having been misidentified in childhood. This could then promise the hypothetical possibility of true transsexuality being recognised. There is no current or foreseeable evidence for this, but not surprisingly, much of the literature on transsexuality concentrates on just this area of sex being developmental in nature, though without recognising the kind of presumptions that are being made, or the depth of difficulty in the project. It appears that in the 'intersex' state of *Joel/Joella* what was encountered was purely a failure of medical discernment. But there seems an eagerness in certain

---

11. See p.58.

quarters to anticipate some future 'discovery' of how the very operation of the developmental characteristics of human life may be shown to affect the 'givenness' of sex, e.g. through presently unknown environmental factors. That is, we are currently, unbeknown to ourselves, subject to sex-development influences, which means that our given sex could be altered in some fashion. It will be apparent from this report that we do not consider it remotely likely that such factors will ever be identified as responsible for causing a 'late intersex' state.[12]

An Additional Consideration

Sometimes the problem of sex/gender alienation is so destructive, or potentially destructive, of the individual that it may be considered that some limited form of intervention be recommended as a proportionate pastoral response.[13] For example, if the co-operation between a transsexual person and his/her counsellors has broken down, and suicide appears the likely result of any refusal to intervene, then forms of intervention may well be pastorally legitimated by the ensuing emergency, though subject to the usual criteria of the minimum necessary. Thus, hormonal treatment may be preferred to surgery, for example, though it should be noted that abuse of this procedure with consequent damaging side effects is not infrequent. This does not rule out the possibility that surgery may be indicated by the pastoral emergency, though the kind of indication that will count here must be extreme. Although a patient may properly decide whether or not to undergo a given treatment, it is, of course, subject to the supposition that the treatment is *prima facie* an appropriate response to the patient's need. It is not an

---

12. Even if such a possibility could one day be established, the case for the essential givenness of sex, as argued in this report, would largely remain unchanged.
13. See pp.80f. for our treatment of this issue as a pastoral dilemma within the context of ecclesiology as distinct from the ethical implications considered here.

undetermined choice, but a personal decision as to how to proceed in the face of a situation of grave necessity. It is no different from other major medical decisions in that respect. The decision whether to undergo transsexual surgery cannot, of course, be correctly described as a choice regarding which sex to be since the fundamental determination of the patient's sex is given, just as the gender dysphoric condition is given.

The Question of Marriage

Within the general ethical debate in relation to transsexuality, a question which often arises concerns what the status of the post-operative transsexual should be with regard to marriage to someone of the opposite body gender characteristics? The answer in the law (of England and Wales), based appropriately enough on the traditional Christian understanding of the special significance of sexual and bodily identity for marriage as the *sole* significance of sexual differentiation, still is (at least for the time being) that one's sex is what is inscribed on one's birth certificate,[14] and that marriage can only be legitimated between a man and a woman. Although this is not the place to enter into a detailed discussion regarding the nature of marriage, it is important to at least to touch upon some of the implications suggested by the above investigations for marriage.

In the case of a person whose sex/gender alienation is regarded as alienation from a true and given sex, it seems to us unlikely that such an individual is in a good position to marry. That is true whether the alienation is acknowledged humbly as estrangement from the true and given (biological) self, or is used as a basis for resentment of the body. If the person *is* married (and most clearly if the marriage is pointed to as the grounds of discovery of the alienation) the pastoral context for the person's

---

14. Hence the significance of the *Joel/Joella* case, where the birth certificate was changed.

sexual being includes the marriage. Of course, Christians will wish to affirm the importance of extending humility to cover respect for the marriage relationship as a given fact of the individual's context, too.[15]

In the event of acceptance of the hypothetical category of genuine late-recognised sex-misidentification (the case for which this study remains highly sceptical), the Christian response will depend upon a variety of factors. The law does not currently allow any such person to marry, because it does not recognise such a situation. Obedience to law implies a present restriction. If it is considered there is no such state as 'late-recognised sex-misidentification', then marriage is obviously impossible to someone of the same sex, and the law is fine as it stands.

If we seek to offer a principled answer for all cases, it would have to be that such people might not marry. In practice, it may be better to say that no blanket principle should be entertained, but principles developed for application to specific cases ought to be discussed. Such discussion would have to take into account the *legal* framework, not least for Anglicans; the Church of England *may* potentially find itself in a position of having to make its churches available for marriage services to those whom it believes unable to marry (for example, as a result of transsexual people being legally able to change their birth certificates and legal identity), which in turn ought to precipitate a reassessment of the legal framework for marriage in the Church of England.

As a concluding comment, it should, perhaps, be recognised that certain of our judgements about marriage might be founded on prejudices which include regarding marriage as the 'best' or 'truest' state of human fulfilment on earth, prejudices which owe more to romanticism in our culture than to Christian tradition. For example, it is evident that we tend somewhat unjustifiably

---

15. The ramifications of possible scenarios where the marriage, as well as the body, are resented are complex and varied, and it is inappropriate in the context of this study to investigate them here. They will include, for example, the question of whether a spouse who has been deserted and divorced by someone who has undergone gender re-alignment should be free to remarry.

to ignore the long and venerable Christian tradition of celibacy or holy virginity.[16]

---

16. The marriage issue is also discussed briefly in the context of celibacy within the pastoral section of this report.

7

Some Practical and Pastoral Considerations Relating to Transsexuality

To distil practical wisdom from the more conceptual nature of the foregoing chapters is not a straightforward task, and in the following section it will not be possible to do full justice to the pastoral consequences of such a complex subject. Neither do we wish or indeed feel able to be dogmatically prescriptive. What we are seeking to do is to consider some of the implications that may arise for Christian groups by the presence of transsexual people, and to offer some general guidelines, which hopefully will prove useful for application in local and specific situations, for the Christian community.

Transsexuality poses significant challenges, both moral and theological, for Christians, and the issues involved often go much deeper than is frequently supposed. A balanced approach that maintains scriptural convictions together with a compassionate response can prove immensely difficult in practice. Transsexual people are fundamentally human beings experiencing deep personal pain and, sadly, transsexuals who wish to join a church, or transsexual Christians who are already members of churches and who seek the support of their church in facing the challenge of potential gender change, may be met on the one hand with blank lack of comprehension or, frequently, on the other hand, with outright hostility. Whilst such responses must not be excused, nevertheless they are understandable given the emotiveness of the subject and the widespread perception of threat posed by transsexuality to fundamental Christian beliefs. Church leaders may find themselves constrained by their members to bring pressure to bear on a transsexual person to conform socially and even to undergo, for example, 'corrective' hormone treatment or psychological re-programming. There have been instances of well-intentioned, but relatively uninformed and insensitive, responses in the shape of healing or deliverance ministry, which have proved disastrous for the individual concerned. It is important to stress that insensitive and ill-advised treatment of a transsexual person can prove devastating and dangerous, sometimes at worst leading to suicide, and at best almost certainly risking driving the person out of the church and into the transsexual 'ghetto'. We wish to emphasise there is no prescriptive 'formula' for dealing with transsexual people. Each person is an individual with a unique personality and history. In the final analysis local responses will be determined by local factors and local pastoral policy. Our aim in this section is to assist in the process of response formulation.

Initial Pastoral Considerations

Pastoral considerations related to transsexual people cannot, of course, be divorced from the debate about origins and causality. An informed counselling approach will be influenced significantly by whether biological or psychological factors are thought to predominate. However, this requires a measure of experience and expert knowledge, and support from sympathetic knowledgeable counsellors, especially informed Christian psychiatrists, will usually be essential at the earliest stages. Frequently, however, such a resource will not be available locally or within the church.

Relatively few instances exist where transsexuals have returned to their former sex-roles following conversion to Christianity.[1]

---

1. See, for example, *Transsexualism in the Church: a Pastor Responds* (Watford: Parakaleo Ministry 1997).

Even so, it is almost certain that special pastoral issues will inevitably be raised by the advent of transsexual people within a church context. It is surely imperative that from the earliest possible moment a church should be able to exercise a positive and encouraging role as a witness to the healing, transforming, restorative power and love of Christ within the Christian community. But equally it is important to receive transsexual people as they are without imposing conformity to supposed Christian behavioural expectations from the outset. Experience has indicated that pastors do well to resist pressure to push a person into any particular course of action, and a very carefully planned programme of therapy, worked out in consultation with experts and with the full co-operation of the church, is vital if the process of ministry to the transsexual person is to be handled responsibly.[2] The process of rehabilitation is usually long and gradual, and care should be taken not to cause damage and distress to a transsexual who is reorienting to their original gender, e.g. by prematurely insisting they dress in accordance with their biological gender.

Specific Challenges

It has been argued that for the Christian, the biblical view of creation as the work of God's sovereignty maintains the sanctity of the distinction between the two sexes. The notion of a given, created, dimorphic humankind, as expressed in the book of Genesis, and the sanctity of a complementary marriage relationship between male and female, is fundamental to Christian thought. The integrity of individual personhood and collective moral responsibility for society is part of the essence of Christian thought and action.

If we believe that redemption and restoration begin within the church community, as fundamental a challenge as trans-

---

2. Ibid.

sexuality is, it nevertheless demands compassion, knowledge and wisdom to respond to it appropriately. At the outset it needs to be appreciated that a church may be faced with transsexual people who are at different stages of transition and consequently have different needs – ranging from people who are unhappy with their sexuality, and transvestites who may be contemplating treatment, to those who have to make a momentous decision about gender reassignment surgery or, indeed, have already undergone surgery. Dealing with a pre-operative transsexual person raises significantly different considerations from a post-operative transsexual. The pre-operative transsexual may typically raise concerns that revolve around marriage and family, and may be anxious to establish whether it is appropriate for surgery to be proceeded with. Tension will exist for all concerned whilst the complex underlying issues remain unresolved. The perceived ambiguity of Scripture and the absence of evident guidelines additionally complicate the consideration process. If surgery does take place, the tension especially for families is not likely to cease, and further practical dilemmas will undoubtedly arise at every turn. The collateral effects for a spouse and children, as well as extended family, are likely to remain long after surgery is completed. Taking male-to-female transsexuals as an example, in almost all cases wives and children want a husband and father who will conform to the norms of what would be seen as a traditional Christian society. Associated issues such as divorce and access to children become major considerations.

It is evident that the implications for the existing marriages of transsexual people are somewhat different depending on whether they are contemplating surgery or whether it has been performed. It is inevitable that particularly difficult pastoral challenges will be involved, especially since grounds for divorce become complex and multi-faceted. Though preservation of Christian marriage remains a high priority, in practice varying views are adopted across the church with regard to the justifiable validity of the associated grounds for separation and divorce, and though experience will inevitably vary from church to church, a sensitive approach is surely what is invariably needed, notwithstanding doctrinal convictions, in offering pastoral advice in the light of actual circumstances.

For the post-operative transsexual, the experience of serious remorse, trauma, and confusion following the euphoric immediate post-operative phase is not uncommon.[3] The transsexual person may in practice not be adequately prepared to deal constructively with a potentially unsympathetic and hostile community. Reverse surgery to replace removed anatomy is not usually available. The transsexual's expectation of acceptance especially by those who biologically belong to the assumed gender may well be disappointed, whilst reactions of those belonging to the opposite assumed gender may be deeply suspicious. Though some post-operative transsexuals are able to adapt amazingly well to their adopted gender, often profound psychological issues remain unresolved by surgery.[4] The transsexual person may, in consequence of both psychological and environmental factors, come to see alienation and distancing from the church and society as the only mutually desirable outcome. Both the pre- and post-operative transsexual may eventually feel compelled to seek out relationships amongst those already outside mainstream society or church, and not infrequently find it necessary to adopt a 'ghetto' type of existence.

It should be appreciated that both the pre- and post-operative transsexual person, having advanced to such a stage, will have done so having become convinced that such a course of action is the only way forward for them. To them probably the only really serious option for resolution to the internal conflict that exists within themselves may well appear to be to seek surgical alteration to the body, thus hopefully conforming it to what they believe themselves to be. Evidently, for the male that means 'female' and 'feminine'. Similarly for female transsexuals who believe they are 'male' and 'masculine'.

---

3. S. Churcher, *The Anguish of the Transsexual* (Lexington: CrossOver Ministries, 1997).
4. Ibid.

Transsexuality and the Church

Transsexuality raises a host of issues for *ecclesiology*. When a transsexual person wishes to enter the church community inevitably a number of pastoral and practical questions arise relating to the basis of their entry and ongoing participation. Difficult questions about whether confidentiality is desirable or possible are raised at the outset. In some cases the presence of a transsexual is obvious to all, whereas there have been situations in which a transsexual has gone undetected for a considerable time. Each particular situation will be different though, of course, normal rules of confidentiality should be applied where possible. Church leaders will require wisdom in knowing how best to handle the issue of whether and how the church should be informed.

Often an early issue to be identified may be the subject of baptism. In principle, it could be argued that there would appear to be some scriptural warrant for allowing baptism of a transsexual, for example, by analogy with the experience of the Ethiopian eunuch's encounter with Philip.[5] Of course, consideration of baptism implies also attention to the associated requirements for repentance, acknowledgement of commitment to obedience to Christ, and acceptance of the disciplinary oversight of the church.

A related issue concerns the question of the permitted extent of membership of the church and how far it is advisable, or indeed possible, for a transsexual person who temporarily or permanently wishes to continue their lifestyle whilst seeking to integrate with the church community. In some churches this question may focus on whether a transsexual is permitted to take communion. Churches will undoubtedly adopt differing views in this regard; for example, some might consider simple attendance to be acceptable, whilst full membership may not be available until appropriate repentance and change are in evidence. Other churches, perhaps

---

5. Acts 8:26–39.

somewhat unwisely, may prefer to ignore the issue, or at the opposite extreme make it clear that the individual is less than welcome. Transsexuality represents an unknown quantity for most churches. Conflicts and suspicions are, regrettably, likely to occur. Unfortunately, any differential treatment of a transsexual person who wishes to play a full part in a church congregation will quickly be sensed and resented by the individual concerned, if the basis for it is not made clear from the outset. In general, we believe that the public promotion of a transsexual lifestyle as a legitimate alternative within a congregational or Christian setting to be inconsistent with biblical teaching, and recognise this may ultimately entail the need for appropriate church disciplinary response. We understand that churches will differ in what they feel is the right course of action given their particular context, but in general we would distinguish between criteria required for church membership, and the compassion Christians would wish to demonstrate to those who, despite counsel, nevertheless determine to pursue apparently sinful behaviours, recognising a distinction between who people *are* and what they *do*. It is appreciated that churches may resolve in extreme situations that those who insist on proceeding with a course of action which Christians view as opposed to the revealed will of God, may render themselves liable to disciplinary measures of the church. However, we would nevertheless affirm ongoing pastoral care to be encouraged where appropriate.

The pastoral and ecclesiological issues surrounding marriage are likely to be even more perplexing. Transsexual people may consider the suggestion of enforced celibacy to be equivalent to a life of unfairly imposed loneliness and therefore may often seek human companionship within the protection of a 'marriage' relationship, should the opportunity arise. It is not uncommon for transsexual people to have persuaded themselves that a church marriage in their assumed gender role is legitimate.[6] Potential

---

6. Though in a recent BBC *Everyman* documentary broadcast on 24th October 1999, an Anglican parish church was willing to bless in church the 'marriage' of a male-to-female transsexual with a female-to-male transsexual.

conflict with firmly held traditional views of church ministers and their members appears inevitable, and complex inter-related issues may be involved including divorce and the responsibility for children. Pastoral counselling in such circumstances will require immense skill, wisdom and compassion if the presence of the person in the church is to be maintained. Ultimately, in addition of course to legal considerations, theological views concerning marriage held by the local church may be determinate of the outcome. It is our view that the church should not be afraid to promote celibacy as a positive alternative life choice, endorsed by both Jesus and Paul in the New Testament.[7] Jesus, though celibate, was the complete and wholly fulfilled human being. It was he who, in an act of self-sacrifice, willingly laid aside divine prerogatives to be an obedient servant. He is the example for irrevocably transsexually (or homosexually) oriented people and millions of heterosexual men and women whom God is not calling to marriage.[8]

A potentially difficult question for church leaders is whether transsexual people should be ordained, or indeed permitted to function in leadership roles within the church.[9] Whilst we are reluctant to impose hard and fast rules, nevertheless it would in principle be clear that, on the basis of biblical passages such as 1 Timothy 3:1–13 and Titus 1:6–9, excellent and unquestioned role models are foundational requirements for Christian leadership. As transsexual people are role models so fundamentally distinct from accepted examples, we consider their appointment to leadership or counselling positions within the church to be

---

[7]. See Matthew 19:1–11 and 1 Corinthians 7:25–38.
[8]. We would like to stress that celibacy by no means necessarily implies loneliness; ministry to transsexuals who live a celibate lifestyle may well involve continuing sensitive recognition of such feelings and other difficulties faced by single people.
[9]. See the *Daily Mail* for 20th and 21st June 2000, for reports relating to the Anglican vicar, Peter Stone, whose bishop 'supposedly' saw no 'legal, ethical or moral' reason to oppose his intended gender reassignment surgery.

unwise on biblical as well as other grounds. Church leaders, however, need to explore ways in which a transsexual person's gifts and abilities can to some extent be recognised so that there is a measure of mutually peaceful integration into the church community. Accordingly, we would oppose the ordination of self-determined transsexual people to ministry or to responsible leadership roles within the church, and we stand prayerfully with those in the churches who believe it is right to resist such moves on biblical grounds. However, we equally would urge churches to consider whether there are ways in which transsexual people who are seeking to reverse change and have been admitted to membership can contribute to the church community in accordance with their gifts.

There are no easy answers to the potential dilemmas posed by the presence of transsexual people in the church context. Any solutions will necessarily involve careful planning and lengthy timescales to permit attitudes and sensitivities on both sides to be accommodated. The fundamental pastoral challenge may be seen as the need to genuinely welcome transsexual people into a caring and compassionate Christian community in which all stand in need of the love, mercy and grace of God, and which recognises that the transsexual person is just as 'human' as anybody else. It should nevertheless be understood that the presence of transsexual people within the body of Christ may unfortunately frequently provoke human reactions of hostility, together with a wide range of concerns which may especially include any perceived impact on the younger members of a church community, where attempts at explanation may be well nigh impossible, let alone offensive and unadvisable. In seeking to welcome transsexual people, Christian communities need to be aware that transsexual individuals typically experience extreme anguish and pain throughout their lifetime. Many people find the process of sanctification long and arduous. It can be particularly laborious for the transsexual who is seeking to resolve inner conflict; the need for patience, long-term commitment and the active seeking of God for wisdom by all concerned cannot be over emphasised.

Ministering to the Transsexual Person in a Church Context

From a Christian perspective, transsexuality may be considered to be an expression of an extreme form of personal alienation and disunity. In practice it can be extremely difficult to counter a core self-belief that has developed typically along the lines, 'God has made a mistake in the way that he has created me'. Years developing an absolute conviction that 'I have been born this way and cannot be cured' may impair the receptivity to the grace and mercy of God that is ultimately necessary to overcome transsexuality. Even if it is accepted that the roots of transsexuality appear to form in early childhood when an awareness of the distinctions between the sexes is first beginning to develop, it can nevertheless be an oversimplification to focus too much pastoral attention on only one or two perceived causes. In reality, causal factors are likely to be numerous. Especially for the male, fantasy can play a major role as a way of 'anaesthetising' personal pain. Following a classic psychological pattern, fantasy may tend to develop into a retreat into false comfort, particularly when stress occurs, as of course it almost always does in life. In time the fantasy may further grow into an addiction or obsession that must be satisfied if life is to be self-fulfilling. Transsexual people often refer to a 'point of no return'. Family, work and social life may all be surrendered in pursuit of what effectively may be seen by outsiders as a self-deception or illusion. Resorting to medical and para-medical opinion is not likely, in many instances, to provide the panacea hoped for. Medical opinion can often be divided and inconclusive. Some advisors (some of whom actually appeal to Christian values of compassion and holistic therapy) may readily counsel gender reassignment surgery in the belief that this will introduce a measure of psychosomatic integrity, judging that it is better to give the individual what he or she wants.

However, many evangelical Christians prefer to offer a Christ-centred holistic psychosomatic approach with the aim of restoration for motivated individuals, focused on a Christ who desires wholeness for all in every aspect of life. This view presupposes an outlook that regards the transsexual 'condition' as one more obvious expression of the dysfunctional nature of humanity, and therefore not to be received without seeking Holy Spirit-aided movement towards acceptance of one's birth sex. It may nevertheless exclude any insensitive and unrealistic expectations and demands that post-conversion transsexual people revert immediately to their original gender. Transsexuality may on this understanding therefore be regarded as a question of *self-identity* rather than as a pseudo-form of same-sex attraction or homosexuality.

In some cases post-operative transsexuals attracted to the church may be unwilling ever to contemplate reversal to their biological sex. For the church to accept such a resolution could be fundamentally problematic since it would appear to involve acquiescence in what many would regard as a serious impediment to the individual's Christian restoration and wholeness. However, we recognise that some churches out of genuine pastoral concern may decide to go along with the new identity in spite of deep-seated misgivings, believing that the best hope for the individual lies in a life of relative integration within the body of Christ where divine grace should be most available. We do not suggest that such an approach is easy. Experience shows that it will require much grace and suspension of judgment from all the members. Not all churches will feel it possible, or even right, to place such a burden on their people. The church may find that one of the most difficult situations arises where a transsexual person in contact with the church, despite every well-intentioned effort to advise them otherwise, comes to the conclusion that the only alternatives open to them are gender reassignment surgery or suicide. Whilst not wishing to condone a course of action believed to be inherently opposed to God's revealed will, the lesser of two evils in such a case may necessarily and unavoidably be seen to be authentic practical support of the transsexual person throughout the operative phase as the only realistic compassionate option.[10] If a church feels unable to contemplate such support and the risk of suicide is considered to be real, realistically and inevitably the involvement of social services would be needed as a last resort.

A church community that acknowledges the skewing of self-identity by the transsexual person will wisely be cautious not to force conformity by insisting on the wearing of culturally appropriate clothing and other social behaviours to 'anticipate' any sanctifying work of the Holy Spirit. As with every Christian, God chooses to work in person-specific ways and we should be careful to allow transsexuals, like everyone else, to 'work out their salvation with fear and trembling'.[11] With regard to everyday life, a transsexual person will need to be encouraged to develop appropriate relational skills in connection with both the male and female members of a church community, notwithstanding the inevitability of certain experienced reactions of hostility and curiosity. The Corinthian church may perhaps serve as a biblical example of a community in which Paul longs for former lifestyles to be dealt with in an appropriately compassionate context. In practice, being able to relate comfortably and appropriately to males may take the male-to-female transsexual time, and the tendency may often be to seek out female companionship. In so doing they are likely to be seeking confirmation of their own perceived form of femininity. Female-to-male transsexuals are sometimes likely to remain distanced from women in a church that they perceive as being overtly 'female'. A wise pastoral response will seek gently to restore the skewed perceptions of a transsexual person to a Biblical view of maleness and femaleness. The pathway of growth, sanctification and change can be expected to be slow and painful. Struggle and relapse can be anticipated.

---

10. This might therefore be viewed as acceptance of SRS as 'a treatment of last resort', however we are reluctant to adopt this as a recommended policy, not least because 'last resort' can easily become a regular response. Our overriding point here is that such a course of action, if supported, would be entirely exceptional.

11. Philippians 2:12.

Total commitment to achieving a personal relationship with a heavenly Father from whom a redeemed sense of gender identity is acquired represents a fundamental, if often long-term, objective.

The transsexual community may view a person desiring to leave the transsexual lifestyle as 'going back', i.e. reverting to a despised former existence. Fellow transsexuals will usually be convinced that change is not possible and sometimes seek to dissuade someone seeking in this way to be obedient to Christ. The process of sanctification should helpfully to be seen by all Christians as a 'new creation' journey – a consistent moving forward in Christ in a positive walk of discovery towards a new and fulfilling life – however long it takes! However, very few will have the resources to undertake such a journey alone.

Conclusion

Affirmations and Recommendations

Across the spectrum of evangelical opinion, we are aware that responses to the contents of this potentially emotive report will vary quite widely. We do not wish to appear prescriptive in this concluding section. We are simply seeking to highlight a series of points that we believe summarise a sensible and mainstream evangelical Christian response to transsexuality. We appreciate that different churches may interpret and apply these guidelines in ways they consider more truly reflect their circumstances and convictions.

1. We recognise that all of us are sinners, and that the only real hope for sinful people, whether heterosexual, homosexual or transsexual, is for wholeness that is to be found only in Jesus Christ. Our earnest prayer is that his love, truth, and grace would characterise evangelical responses to debates about transsexuality and in dealings with transsexual people, both now and in the future.
2. We affirm God's love and concern for all humanity, but believe that God creates human beings as *either* male *or* female. Authentic change from a person's given sex is not

possible and an ongoing transsexual lifestyle is incompatible with God's will as revealed in Scripture and in creation. We would oppose recourse to gender reassignment surgery as a normal valid option for people suffering from gender dysphoria on a biblical basis. We note, in addition, that no long-term research exists to validate the effectiveness of such surgery in effecting gender change. Rather, we believe that acceptance of the gospel of Jesus Christ affords real opportunities for holistic change in the context of non-surgical solutions. We appeal to the medical and psychiatric professions to prioritise research for the purposes of holistic treatment into the root psychological, social, spiritual, and physical causes of 'transsexuality'. This we regard as preferential to the development of technical cosmetic surgical options that remain essentially irreversible and require lifetime recourse to hormone therapy. We appeal to society as a whole to use Christian community values of love and care as a basis for thought and action.

3. We deeply regret any hurt caused to transsexual men and women by any unwelcoming or rejecting attitudes on the part of the church. We call upon evangelical congregations genuinely to welcome and accept transsexual people, whilst acknowledging the need for parallel teaching, wisdom and discernment, especially where children are concerned. Within the context of a loving Christian environment, we hope and anticipate that transsexual people will come in due course to accede to the need to reorient their lifestyle in accordance with biblical principles and orthodox church teaching. We urge gentleness and patience in this process, and ongoing care even following gender reorientation.

4. We affirm that monogamous heterosexual marriage is the form of partnership uniquely intended by God for sexual relationships between men and women. We would oppose moves within some church circles to accept or endorse sexually active transsexual partnerships where the partners are of the same biological sex as legitimate forms of Christian

relationship. Additionally, we would resist church services for the marriage or blessing of transsexual partnerships on scriptural grounds, whether the partners are of the same biological sex or not.

5. We commend and encourage those transsexual Christian people who have determined to restore their birth sex identity as a consequence of biblical conviction, and/or who have decided to resist gender reassignment surgery. We would seek prayerfully to support their reorientation through the grace of God. We further commend and encourage those transsexual Christian people who are willing, but do not yet feel able, to readopt their birth sex identity, but who nevertheless have committed themselves to chastity and celibacy. We affirm celibacy to be an honourable and fulfilling vocation for those whom God has not called to marriage.

6. We prayerfully affirm and encourage those family members who are subjected to the impact of transsexuality. We would seek to support them pastorally in coming to terms with the consequences of a declared transsexual partner, parent, or other relative.

7. We commend the work of those organisations, pastoral workers and churches that seek to help and support transsexual people who face the traumas of loneliness, psychiatric treatment, gender reorientation and gender reassignment surgery.

8. We in principle are opposed to civil discrimination against transsexual people, for example in respect of human rights and employment. However, it is recognised that in practice, particular circumstances may make the continuing position of a transsexual extremely difficult whether or not he or she was in the process of transition.

9. Notwithstanding the arguments in favour, we nevertheless believe the case for transsexual people to be allowed to amend their birth certificates (except in those rare 'intersex'

cases involving genuine medical mistake) to be fundamentally flawed, open to abuse, and tending to undermine accepted realities by condoning illusion and denial. In particular, we believe it would lead to unacceptable legitimisation of currently illegitimate 'marriage' relationships, and remove protection against deception.

Select Bibliography and Further Reading

CHURCHER, SHARON, *The Anguish of the Transsexual* (Watford: Parakaleo Ministry)

DAINTON, MARK and TILLER, KEITH, *'Male and Female He Created Them': Ministry to the Gender Confused* (Watford: Parakaleo Ministry)

HOLDER, RODNEY, 'The Ethics of Transsexualism', in *Crucible,* April–June, 1998, pp.89-9, and July–September 1998, pp.125–36

HORTON, DAVID, *Changing Channels? A Christian Response to the Transvestite and Transsexual* (Grove Ethical Studies No.92, Nottingham: Grove Books, 1994)

KOLAKOWSKI, VICTORIA S., 'Towards a Christian Ethical Response to Transsexual Persons', in *Theology and Sexuality,* No.6, March, 1997, pp.10–23

O'DONOVAN, OLIVER, *Transsexualism and Christian Marriage* (Grove Ethical Studies No.48, Nottingham: Grove Books, 1982)

Overcoming Transsexuality: A Christian Testimony (Watford: Parakaleo Ministry)

Transsexualism in the Church: A Pastor Responds (Watford: Parakaleo Ministry)

WHITEHEAD, N.E. and WHITEHEAD, B.K., *My Genes Made Me Do It!* (Lafayette, Louisiana: Huntington House 1999)

Useful Addresses of Christian Organisations

Parakaleo Ministry (a ministry of Youth with a Mission, London)
Box 115, Bromley, BR1 2ZA.
Telephone: 01782 720994
Fax: 0208 769 7290
E-mail: parakaleo@btinternet.com
Web Page: www.parakaleo.co.uk